English and Its Teaching

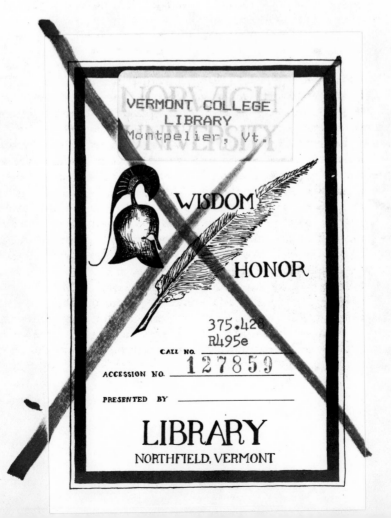

THE PROFESSIONAL EDUCATION SERIES

Walter K. Beggs, *Editor*
Dean Emeritus, Teachers College, and
Professor of Educational Administration
University of Nebraska

Royce H. Knapp, *Research Editor*
Regents Professor of Education
University of Nebraska

English and Its Teaching

by

FRANK M. RICE

Professor of English
and
Co-Director of the Nebraska
Curriculum Development Center
University of Nebraska

PROFESSIONAL EDUCATORS PUBLICATIONS, INC.
LINCOLN, NEBRASKA

Library of Congress Catalog Card No.: 72-77983

ISBN   0-88224-004-8

Contents

Contents

CHAPTER 1

On Becoming a Teacher of English

English and Its Teaching is addressed to the student who is preparing to teach English in the secondary school or to the young teacher who is in his first years of teaching. If the reader belongs to one of these two categories, it is not presumptuous to infer that he is a person who has always found literature interesting and entertaining: he has read widely in short stories, novels, essays, dramas, and poems. He has been fascinated by the process of finding out the origin of many of the common words in our language, the ways such words have changed through several centuries, and the meanings at which they have arrived in our own times. He is a person who has always liked to manipulate words, to add affixes to roots in order to discover in how many ways the same basic word can serve our expressive purposes. He has also been and remains a person who liked to string words together in sentences, who contemplates the choices which he has when he attempts to assemble words in sentence patterns. He also has found delight in grouping sentences into larger elements, such as the paragraph or stanza, the short story, or the ballad. He has known occasions when he would rather sit down quietly and convert his thoughts to written expression than to communicate them orally. He enjoys the possibilities which thoughtfulness and experimentation give him to be clear and graceful in his written communication. If these sentences reflect your nature fairly accurately, then it appears that you are "hooked"; you are most likely to get your greatest satisfaction from teaching English.

Perhaps you should be told — if you have not already anticipated this fact — that a commitment to teaching English is a commitment for life. Particularly is this true if you aspire to be well informed in your discipline and highly skillful in interesting young people in it. The field of literature from its beginning to the mid-twentieth century is vast, and much that is currently being written is exciting, fascinating, and prolific. Thus, the person who would teach English must know a

7

good deal about the background of literature, a knowledge which can be obtained only by reading, reading, and even more reading. Furthermore, if the teacher of English would gain the respect of his students, he needs also to be acquainted with what is being written during the present year. This does not mean that he can limit his knowledge only to that literature which promises to have enduring quality. He must also be at least superficially aware of some of the best sellers. For example, *Love Story* recently created a considerable splash. Many young people thought it to be a literary masterpiece. No wise teacher would dampen the enthusiasm of such young people. On the other hand, no thoughtful teacher would place *Love Story* among those which have endured. What the teacher needs to do, of course, is to find another work of literary merit with which to contrast the current and popular story. Perhaps the study of *A Farewell to Arms* or *Wuthering Heights* would achieve such an objective, and the process would be an educational one for the students. Such a study tends to sharpen the critical faculties of the young and to increase their ability to recognize an honest and moving literary work. It also helps the teacher to realize more efficiently the goals which he would reach as a teacher.

Many school systems have expected the teacher of English to be capable of performing a great many tasks and have asked the teacher to assume responsibility for them. School administrators are themselves often the victims of the community's wishes. When the community imposes an additional educational task on the school, the administrator often passes it on to the English teacher because he and his colleagues are the teachers most likely to have all of the students of the school in their classes. Essay contests, unless they are too restrictive, may be the English teacher's responsibility; but when it comes to teaching the harm inherent in drug addiction or cigarette smoking, this is clearly the responsibility of the total school and community and not the specific responsibility of the teacher of English. The variety of extraneous topics and duties assigned to the English classroom and its teacher have, at least until recently, been legion. In one instance a school made driver-training a part of the English curriculum and the English teacher's responsibility.

The English teacher must know what legitimately is within his purview and should jealously and zealously work to keep his teaching field clearly defined and to understand what his responsibilities should be. Beginning teachers are often intimidated by experienced teachers or administrators and find themselves burdened with obligations which do not seem quite appropriate for the English classroom. The beginning teacher needs to be cooperative, of course, but when he discovers that he is having obligations not rightfully those of an English classroom imposed upon him and his classes, he should object. He is doing the profession a disservice whenever he allows anyone to dilute his discipline or to place it in a second-class position in the school.

Let us consider briefly what components legitimately constitute the discipline of English and what the English teacher's responsibilities are. First: The English teacher should be familiar with a wide range of literary works. He should be familiar with the classical backgrounds of Western literature, the literature of England in its origin, and American literature. And in a world growing increasingly small, he should know something of the literature in translation of other cultures: French, Italian, Russian, Scandinavian, Spanish, etc., particularly that of the past 100 years. Furthermore the teacher should be knowledgeable about the English language with its American variations. He should, of course, know the history of his language, its origin and changes. He should know something about the sound of his language, the relationship between sounds and their graphemic representations. He should have an educated view of dialectology. He should also have studied semantics, word forms, and syntax. If the teacher is a product of a secondary school which taught him traditional (Latinate English) grammar, and if he has never in his higher education learned what a scientific description of the English language has to tell him, he should seek, as soon as possible, to rectify this omission from his training. He should try to study — on his own if no class is available — at least one kind of modern English grammar. Just as no teacher within a lifetime has the time to know in detail the whole field of literature, no teacher has the time either to know all that may be learned about the English language. For too many years schools have taught a Latin-derived grammar of English with its multiplicity of exceptions to rules to the total confusion of approximately 75 percent of the students. A beginning teacher should be aware of the wrongheadedness of textbooks which persist in dealing with this kind of grammar, he should avoid using them, and he should teach only that which is demonstrably true about the English language. The best place for the teacher and his students to look at the way grammar functions is to examine its use in literature.

For a good many years schools have preached that unless a student knows his grammar, he cannot learn to write. This, of course, is sheer nonsense. When Chaucer, Shakespeare, and Milton were composing great literature, there was no written English grammar in existence, not even an inaccurate one. Schools have also confused grammar and usage, the one relevant to structure and the other to matters of propriety, the two never comfortably interchangeable. For example, in a simple sense, grammar has to do with word form and patterns of sentences; usage has to do with appropriateness of word choice, of vocabulary items, to be used as the speaker or writer addresses a particular audience or reader. The beginning teacher needs to understand these distinctions and to be alert to their implications in his own choice of language curriculum and teaching strategy.

Another misconception nurtured by the schools and still persisting in some is the idea that language is taught primarily as a skill and that its value as a subject is inferior to that of literature. Traditional language texts prepared for the secondary school have, over several decades, tended to narrow the field of language teaching; it is for this reason that the school often thinks of the teaching of language as not quite so important as the teaching of literature. However, contemporary linguists have been making us aware of how broad and complex a field the study of language is. Actually the teacher in training or in his first years of teaching should begin to think of the study of language as a humane, cultural subject. For students of a certain disposition the language field is extremely exciting and attractive. The beginning teacher should be aware of this fact and capitalize on it to the advantage of the student and to the enlarging of his own pleasure. Language study may be comprised of three broad areas: meaning, which can involve one in a study of vocabulary, etymology, and semantics—how words come to mean what they do; form, which involves the student in an awareness of how affixes of one kind or another determine in what ways words function and in an awareness of sentence slots and the words which normally fit these slots, and, even more importantly, in an understanding of the facility with which words may be manipulated to create a variety of sentence patterns; and finally sound, as it bears on our understanding of our writing system, the graphemic (spelling) representations of language sounds, on the supra-segmental features of the language, such as matters of pitch, stress, and juncture and how punctuation serves to represent these, and also sound as it bears upon dialectal variations and upon English prosody—rhythm and rhyme patterns in poetry. Here is a wide field for the beginning teacher; and it may be a field partially or totally unknown to the beginner. If this is the situation, the teacher has some deprivations in training to overcome.

The beginning teacher should not be ashamed of the limitations in his training in language, but should proceed modestly teaching what he knows to be true and, by attending summer school, extension classes, or by doing personal reading he can continue to increase his understanding of the language. As he informs himself, so will he inform his students. Both the teacher and his students should come to see what a miraculous phenomenon language is.

Another bonafide responsibility of the English teacher is to teach students how to write, how to translate their oral language into the written. Few people really know very much about how this is done or whether it is really possible for a teacher to teach young people how to write clearly, effectively, and appropriately. Some young people seem to have an instinctive understanding of the process and compose essays, stories, and poems of an excellence which their teachers are unable to explain or to equal; whereas other young people, intelligent and capable in many respects, can scarcely string three or four sentences together in a meaningful and logical sequence.

The English teacher is not likely to find a process of instruction which will teach all of this students to write well, but he can do a number of things which will help the class toward such a goal. First, the teacher should try to create an environment in which writing is encouraged and the student is motivated to write. Sometimes this means creating a relaxed and natural environment in which students can first talk freely and easily before writing. The teacher must always be positive and never negative; he should always find some element in a student's writing to praise and should be exceedingly careful not to emphasize the flaws. Furthermore, the teacher has to earn the confidence of the student. The student has to feel that he can express his most honest thoughts without fear of being derided or belittled. Finally, the teacher needs to engage the student in a genuinely thoughtful experience and stimulate his emotions to the point where he enjoys and becomes unable to resist expressing his feelings. Thinking and feeling strongly about a subject are ways of generating quality composition among the young. Teachers who impose superficially considered topics on students for composition purposes are likely to get in return exactly what they deserve, artificial and superficial composition. The composition assignment has to be very thoughtfully created. To tell students in haste that they will be expected to turn in a 500-word composition the next day on such inadequate topics as "My most enjoyable day last summer," "My most embarrassing moment," etc., is to make failure sure.

The study of literature is a very natural context within which genuine writing can be generated. In addition to becoming intellectually and emotionally involved with a literary selection, the student may also have his attention called to the form which the professional writer has used, not only the overall form but also the structures of his sentences and paragraphs, verses or stanzas. Exercises in which the teacher and his students experiment with making changes in the author's structure often teach young people how much thought goes into getting the writing pattern just right. Such exercises also tend to open up to young people a sense of the choices they have from which to choose as they pattern their oral composition in writing.

There is nothing new under the sun, so to speak. Most of the writing of contemporary writers is simply variations upon the forms created by earlier writers. Originality is the personality of an individual writer superimposed upon what is very often a traditional model. Therefore, another way by which the beginning teacher can encourage the young writer to write is to call his attention to models which the literature which he is currently studying happens to exhibit. For the teacher and student to look together at the detailed characteristics of a particular model is to help both to improve their writing.

A teacher should seldom ask students to do a writing assignment which he is unwilling to do himself. It is easy for a teacher to ask for a particular writing assignment from students but, asked to fulfill the same assignment himself, he may find it a difficult if not an impossible task to perform. An English teacher should be himself a writer. Even if he writes with no idea of trying to get published, he should continue to write. Only by continuous writing do we discover the variety of ways our ideas may be communicated—an understanding which we can also pass on to our students—but also the experience is likely to teach us a kind of humility. It makes us aware of the writing assignments which we impose upon our students and the peculiar difficulties which each may pose. By becoming conscious of such difficulties, we are in a better position to help those students for whom the task may be unconventionally difficult.

This introductory chapter has been written primarily as a means of helping a teacher in training or a beginning teacher of secondary-school English to determine whether this is truly the subject which he believes he wants to teach as a career, to alert him to what comprises the discipline which he would practice, and to comment on some of the important aspects of literature, language, and composition—the three components of most English programs.

This chapter indicated some of the recent developments in our understanding of and knowledge about literature, language, and composition. The following chapters treat each of these components more fully, discussing the new developments of each which have occurred during the past decade. The following chapter will sketch briefly what the state of English was before 1960; the final chapter will call attention to a miscellany of subjects, all of which should be relevant to the beginning teacher. Hopefully, this introduction has given the reader a sense of his career challenges and opportunities in teaching English in the secondary school. Hopefully, it has also sensitized him to the responsibilities and commitments which such a career poses.

CHAPTER 2

The Revolt Against Traditional English Programs

If the reader was a secondary-school student during the nineteen-sixties, he may have been affected by some of the changes which were taking place in the English curriculum and by some of the experimental strategies which teachers of English were using in their classrooms during that decade. But if the reader completed his public school education in the nineteen-fifties, he may recall that he studied a somewhat stagnant curriculum taught by a mild type of drillmaster. Rote learning of this sort has persisted even to the present in some culturally inactive pockets in this country. The reader may have been drilled in prescriptive grammar and expected to study literature as artifacts of genius, to be admired but seldom enjoyed. He may also have been taught literature as a combination of biography and history rather than as an art form. Before 1960 the study of literature and language bore too little relevance to the temper of the nation in the mid-century or to the young people caught up in a culture growing increasingly complicated and contradictory.

The Russians' launching of Sputnik usually has had attributed to it the sudden and rather wholesale reexamination of the schools' curriculum which the United States undertook. Although mathematics and the physical sciences were the first subjects to be scrutinized, because of its dominant role in the curriculum of the secondary school, English soon followed. Since that time the English curriculum and the training programs of those who would teach English have been in a state of ferment.

What was the nature of the secondary-school English curriculum before Sputnik? The two mainstays of the curriculum were a series of literature anthologies and a series of language-composition books. Perhaps the programs for training teachers of English had been unrealistic, inadequate, and generally superficial because teachers as

14

group were willing to let commercial publishers of such textbooks decide what should comprise their curriculum. It is true, of course, that some experienced teachers were selective and used the literature anthologies only in part and where they found them of value and often left the language-composition books sitting on their cupboard shelves. But far more teachers accepted the adopted anthology and used it religiously and completely even with all of its shortcomings. They also continued to drill students on the rules of traditional grammar and used the irrelevant composition exercises of the language-composition series *ad nauseum*. Reform in English was imminent.

One of the events which stimulated reform in the creation of teaching materials was the publication in 1959 of James J. Lynch and Bertrand Evans' *High School English Textbooks: A Critical Examination* (New York: The Ronald Press). These writers called to the attention of teachers, as well as publishers, the notorious inadequacies of the major literature anthologies and grammar-composition books used in American schools. In this same publication, Irving Gersten, "Introduction and Summation," objected to the "excessive reliance upon a spate of non-literary, non-fictional, 'informational' materials more suitable at their best to the daily newspaper than to a hard-covered, sturdily constructed anthology with a presumed claim to longevity exceeding twenty-four hours." Gersten concluded they were particularly critical of the "solicitous urge to make anthologies 'easier' and thus more palatable to 'reluctant' and other readers who might otherwise shy away from more substantial challenges to their intelligence, sensitivity, and endurance, and give up reading altogether."

Lynch and Evans found anthologies "over-organized" and full of "extensive introductions and other editorial machinery" which "overwhelms to the point of obliteration the puny examples to which they address themselves." The authors also found severe fault with the senseless abridgment of poems and plays which gave students an incomplete acquaintance with certain literary selections.

Lynch and Evans also pointed out a serious fault evident in the language-composition series. Not only was the grammar an outmoded one, but each book in the series, sometimes as many as six, presented the same materials so that students using these series would be bored almost to extinction by the time they had been forced through them for two to four repetitions.

Indirectly, what Lynch and Evans revealed was an indictment of both the programs by which English teachers had been trained and the inadequacies of English teachers who used the anthologies and other textbooks without protest.

In the 1930s a prominent high school in a midwestern city employed two English department chairmen to supervise the teaching of English. One was in charge of the literature department and the other in charge of the language-composition department. The literature department conducted its program with no more than superficial reference to the language-composition department, and the reverse was true. It was the language-composition teacher's responsibility to teach freshmen descriptive writing, sophomores narrative composition, and juniors expository composition. In the senior year students might elect creative writing or, if their achievement in their first three years was worthy, they might be excused from composition during their final year. In each year students alternated a semester of the study of literature with a semester of the study of language-composition. This was one of the high schools which was included in the report of James R. Squire and Roger K. Applebee, *A Study of English Programs in Selected High Schools Which Consistently Educate Outstanding Students in English.*

This particular program represents, in a sense, how far wrong even a very good school could go in providing a viable English program. The school was a good school because it drew its students from a community largely settled by professional people. These students, inner-directed, succeeded in spite of the curriculum. They were quite the opposite of contemporary students who demand knowing why courses are structured as they are and will protest strongly against any program that seems nonsensical to them or irrelevant to their lives.

Looking at the English program of this "good" school, one can see how ridiculous its program actually was. One knows now that literature affords the teacher and student excellent opportunities to observe language used at its best, and by *best* one means honestly, appropriately, and effectively used. One also knows that to create an artificial context in which good composition can be generated is almost an impossibility. Literature has the power to lay hold of the reader's intellect and to quicken and intensify his emotional responses. Any number of literary selections, either prose or poetry, can motivate young people to respond — to agree or disagree, to scorn or praise. Giving young people a situation in which they have a strong impulse to express their ideas is at least one step toward developing composition ability. Thus to structure an English program in which literature, language, and composition are taught as discrete areas is to fail to take advantage of the mutual motivation which the three studied together can generate. A teacher can begin class with the

study of a particular literary selection. As the class reads and dis-
cusses this selection, the clever teacher can point out vocabulary
items which are effective, discuss the dialog as a representation of a
particular kind of dialect—that of the highly educated, the immature,
the poor white, the black, the foreign-born, etc.—and discuss its appropriateness. The teacher can also get students interested in examining the syntax of the selection, asking them to look at the manner in
which the writer has patterned his sentences, asking them to create
model sentences of their own on the patterns which they have noted,
or asking them to experiment with syntax by rearranging the patterns
of the professional writer to see whether they can improve on them.
The teacher can also engage the young people with an examination
of, and experimentation with, more elaborate patterns—those of paragraphs, short stories, essays, narrative or lyric poems, dramas. This
manner of integrating the three components of English within the
same lesson is growing especially widespread in England and is getting well started in the United States. Because of their faith in a program which interrelates the areas of literature, language, and
composition, the British participants at the Dartmouth Conference
(discussed more fully in Chapter 6) tended to reject some of the
highly structured programs which had been developed at the English
curriculum study centers and funded by the United States Office of
Education. In some instances, of course, they overlooked the fact
that some of these programs separated the three areas only superficially as a means of making it easier to explain each even though,
within each, the teacher is encouraged to be on the alert for those
junctures which naturally encourage looking at language in a literary
context and by developing composition in a literary and language
context.

The profession itself was aroused from an academic lethargy in
the late nineteen-fifties, and the early nineteen-sixties saw it engaged
with an examination of the curriculum materials being offered in
American high schools and the pedagogic stance which English
teachers took. George Winchester Stone, executive secretary of the
Modern Language Association, and J. N. Hook, then executive secretary of the National Council of Teachers of English, as well as other
scholars and teachers, were responsible for initiating discussions of
the discipline on a nationwide basis. These scholars, some 28 of them,
attempted to formulate the Basic Issues in English Curriculum and
the preparation of English teachers, in a book entitled *The Basic
Issues in the Teaching of English.* The group stated: "Our only vested
interest is the development of an increasingly higher degree of

literacy in young American citizens. We think the matter is urgent; we hope that the profession will see these issues as basic and will expeditiously find solutions for the problems arising from them."

This group affirmed their belief in an English curriculum which is both sequential and cumulative in nature, practically and socially useful, and "permanently rewarding to the mind and spirit of those who are fortunate enough to get it." Too, Jerome S. Bruner's *The Process of Education* emphasized the necessity that programs worthy of the name would be sequential and of a spiraling nature. From the Basic Issues group came a statement of what constitutes the core of English. The group defined it as being comprised of three areas: the study of literature, language, and of composition. In view of the amorphous character which the discipline had degenerated to during World War II, this definition was a step in the right direction. Teachers of English had become unsure of what their areas and responsibilities were.

The Commission on English of the College Entrance Examination Board, ably served by Floyd Rinker as executive secretary, produced a significant report in 1965, *Freedom and Discipline in English.* This report explained that "language, primarily the English language, constitutes the core of the subject." This report also recommended "that the scope of the English program be defined as the study of language, literature, and composition, written and oral, and that matters not clearly related to such study be excluded from it." Truly professional teachers of English in the secondary school now had reassurance of what they had all along suspected to be their areas of teaching responsibility, since such areas had been signified by the best scholars of the profession, and they were able to defend their positions from the assaults of administrators who lacked respect for their academic individuality and would have them be all things to all students.

In 1961 The National Council of Teachers of English published the influential book, *The National Interest and the Teaching of English,* which outlined seven important goals:

> To focus instruction in English upon the study of language, literature and composition.
> To educate teachers of English to the developmental and sequential nature of the study and to institute a national program for encouraging articulation of English studies throughout the school years.
> To improve present preparatory programs for teachers of English.

To improve the preparation of practicing teachers of English.

To improve the services and supplies available to teachers of English.

To encourage scientific research about the teaching of English.

To recruit and prepare more teachers of English.

It is interesting, retrospectively, to see how each of these goals served to guide various kinds of professional and federally funded undertakings during the remaining years of the nineteen-sixties.

In 1964 The National Council of Teachers of English prepared a second volume focused on the national interest and English education. This was called *The National Interest and the Continuing Education of Teachers of English.* One achievement of this publication was to point out that literacy in English was as necessary to the national defense as was literacy of scientific and technological kinds. This book was influential in getting Congress in the following spring to enlarge the National Defense Education Act to include English as a field to be improved through the reeducation of teachers of English. One surprising statistic, which was included in this publication, was that 49.5 percent of all secondary-school teachers who conducted English classes at that time in the high schools of the nation lacked majors in English, one third of them (32.8%), in fact, lacked even a college major in a field related to English, such as speech or journalism.

In its budget for 1961 the United States Office of Education received funds to support institutions of higher education interested in creating new and more viable English curricula. Then in 1965 the Office of Education supported several summer institutes for the retraining of teachers of English. By means of these two activities several of the seven goals defined in *The National Interest and the Teaching of English* were being dealt with.

Another of these goals, defined in 1961, was the center of interest at a conference held at the Carnegie Institute of Technology in May of 1962. Their report, *Needed Research in the Teaching of English,* prepared by Erwin R. Steinberg, was concerned with several areas of ignorance which existed in the discipline of English and undertook to define those areas, and, in a sense, to suggest the need for and the directions toward which research in English would proceed in the years immediately following.

To gain a sense of the excitement which was generated during the nineteen-sixties respecting the teaching of English and the training of English teachers, the neophyte or beginning teacher of English should read these books. They impart an excitement about the discipline and its disciples which is inspiring. At the same time there are paragraphs and whole chapters which are still eminently useful and should be meaningful to the person wanting to be informed. There are other books which the young teacher will want to read: to give him a sense of the history of change in his discipline and to help him establish a professional stance for the future. Some of these books will be mentioned in this and succeeding chapters; others will be listed in chapter-end bibliographies. For example, a second publication by the Commission on English of the College Entrance Examination Board, *Speaking about Teaching,* published in 1967 and containing 13 chapters, each by an authority, has a store of relevant information for the person training to become an English teacher. These essays grew out of experiences which a number of observant professionals had in connection with the Commission on English sponsored summer institutes.

Jerome R. Bruner's *The Process of Education* also had a strong effect on the professionals involved in the shaping of new English curricula. Appearing as it did in 1960 as a report which emerged from a conference of 35 scientists and educators at Woods Hole, Cape Cod, who were concerned with ways to improve the teaching of science in the schools, it was taken up by those creating new English curricula, since Bruner had declared that literature as well as the sciences and social sciences could be taught with an emphasis upon the intuitive grasp of ideas and upon the basic ideas. Bruner maintained that the foundations of any subject may be taught to anybody at any age in some form. He also believed that good teaching emphasizes the structure of a subject, and he defended the theory that we should initially teach the student not a skill but an idea which then can become the basis for recognizing subsequent problems as special instances of the idea originally learned. This approach was in clear opposition to a theory which had supported much of the teaching in the schools — the drilling of students on facts and techniques.

With this popular psychological-philosophical theory circulating among educators, it was only natural that English teachers should find useful Northrop Frye's ideas as specific applications to literature of the Bruner theory. In his *Anatomy of Criticism,* written a few years earlier but not well known by public school educators, Frye had suggested that the literature curriculum might be organized by "pre-generic" forms and defined these as comedy, romance, tragedy, and irony. Frye's belief was that it was possible to work out a curriculum which would treat literature as a progressive and systematic study, from grade one to graduate school, that it would be foolish to try to patch up the then existent English curricula typically taught in American schools; and that it was the teacher's obligation to encourage an inductive process which fosters in the student a confidence in his powers to express himself so that his listener or reader will understand what he means. Frye recommended that comedy and romance be taught in the earlier years of schooling and tragedy and irony in the later. Frye's theories gave a good many people working with the development of new English curricula a viable blueprint by which to build a detailed curriculum in literature. How some groups used Professor Frye's theories in the development of English curricula will be more fully discussed in a later chapter, particularly when the literature curriculum developed at the Nebraska Curriculum Development Center is described.

Early in the present century the average student completed the eighth grade and then joined the labor forces of his community while the more able went on to high school. However, more and more elementary-school graduates began going on to secondary school. The enforcement of state laws respecting school attendance had something to do with the increase in the secondary-school population, but even more so this increase was a product of a world growing more complex and demanding better educated citizens. From a time when only 30 to 40 percent of the elementary-school population enrolled in the secondary school has come a time when as many as 90 to 99 percent continue to high school. As a result the secondary-school clientele has become diversified. In addition to those inner-directed young people who attend high school as a step on their way to college or the professional school, there are still a considerable number who terminate their formal education when they reach age sixteen or graduate from grade twelve. Among the latter group are slow learners, economically and culturally deprived students, members of minority groups to whom the curriculum of the school appears to have little relevance. For example, very few American Indian or Chicano students graduate from American high schools.

Since schools are notoriously slow to change, most schools, even as recently as 1960, had not provided a meaningful curriculum in English for the slow learner, the economically or culturally deprived, or the students from minority groups. During the nineteen-sixties a real effort began to provide relevant English curricula for these exceptional students, and a few teacher-training institutions began to prepare teachers to teach these kinds of students. The nineteen-sixties saw a start, while the nineteen-seventies are witnessing a continuing and expanding concern for such students and for the preparation of teaching materials which are relevant to, and teachers who understand how to deal with, such students. The old curriculum was directed toward a mythical average student and was, perhaps, satisfactory in the secondary school when its student body was somewhat select. But where curricula have not changed to provide a meaningful educational experience for the changing character of the student body, the rate of attrition has been high, and the schools have come under attack. A young teacher may very well be assigned during his first years to those schools in a city where there is a preponderance of exceptional students. And he must, therefore, be aware of their presence and should attempt to inform himself as quickly as possible in regard to the kinds of curricula which will succeed and the kinds of understandings which he must have if he is to do an effective job with these students.

The change in the school clientele, new understandings which have come to us from research, new ideas which scholars concentrating on curriculum improvement have enunciated, the federal government's support of the English profession generally—these represent the circumstances and events which began in the nineteen-sixties and which have shown us how outmoded the old English curriculum was and how inadequate was the training of English teachers. These defects or inadequacies in English programs and in the training of people who teach English are being faced and, in some cases, are being overcome. In the next chapters as we shall concern ourselves with some of the changes which have come about during the past decade and with which the beginning teacher, if he would become effective, must acquaint himself.

CHAPTER 3

New Developments in Literature Curricula and Their Teaching

Among many things which the Lynch and Evans' study made evident to members of the English profession were three especially significant ones: literature anthologies as a whole were comprised of snippets, cuttings from longer selections which were insufficient to give students a sense of their individuality and power; literature anthologies furthermore tended to contain far too many contemporary *Reader's Digest* type articles, primarily non-literary in nature, and too few really first-rate literary selections; and finally literature anthologies also tampered with original texts, and in the process of making the selection easier to read, anthology editors diminished or actually destroyed the unique character and style of the original. These deficiencies in the anthologies being widely used over most of the United States alerted those who became engaged with the creation of new literature curricula to these defects and served to keep them from making the same or similar kinds of blunders. The Lynch and Evans' study also served as a guide to the commercial publishers in the improvement of their publications. As a result a good many of the anthologies produced since by commercial publishers have improved.

1962 saw the inception of the English Program of the United States Office of Education, often called informally *Project English.* A number of universities applied for funds to support research in the development of English curriculum materials, and the United States Office of Education funded a significant number. Among the first six were Carnegie-Mellon University (then the Carnegie Institute of Technology), Hunter College of the City of New York, the University of Minnesota, Northwestern University, the University of Nebraska, and the University of Oregon. Some of these curriculum study centers concentrated only on language, or composition, or literature curricula, and a few worked with the three components in combination. One school first prepared curriculum materials only for the college-bound, whereas another had as its audience the disadvantaged. Some centers developed materials for only a three-year sequence; others for a six-year—either grades one-six or seven-twelve; while one center attempted to prepare a curriculum for the total range of the public schools, grades one through twelve, and combined the three components, literature, language, and composition.

In this chapter it will be our purpose to examine some of the more prominent of these programs in order that the teacher in training or the inexperienced teacher may become at least superficially acquainted with these programs which departed from traditional programs and prepared materials of substantial qualities which reflected what research had begun to discover about how to structure programs. These new programs tended to accommodate themselves to the real nature of the young people attending our schools and to be concerned with attracting to, and honestly engaging such students with, the study of English. To help us see these programs somewhat more clearly, we will deal with a single aspect in this chapter and in the next two, discussing what contributions the Office of Education English Program has made, first, to the literature curriculum, second to the language, and third to the composition. In this chapter, then, we shall look at the varieties of curricula in literature which were developed at the most productive of the centers. The four centers were Carnegie-Mellon, Hunter College, University of Nebraska and the University of Oregon.

Let us consider the Carnegie-Mellon curriculum first. Carnegie selected a somewhat limited sequence, one for grades ten-twelve. At first Carnegie developed an integrated program in language, literature, and composition for the bright students who had college participation as a goal. The major purpose of its literature program was to train students to read literature "with understanding and sensitivity." Once this curriculum was completed, Carnegie went on to revise it so that it might also be suitable for students of average ability, students in some cases for whom a high school education would be terminal.

The Carnegie Center believed that the core of a good English program should be literature and that the study of language and composition should be built around this core. Its working definition was that literature is "mankind's record, expressed in verbal art forms, of what it is to be alive." In the tenth grade the literature curriculum concentrates on a variety of universal human concerns: love, heroism, human weakness, and the search for wisdom. In the eleventh grade the Carnegie program attempts to show how these universal concerns are modified by the culture pattern of America, from Puritan times to the present. This one-year curriculum offers schools a vastly improved course in American literature conventionally taught in the eleventh year and concentrating far more on the biographies of authors and the historical aspects of the several periods than on the literature itself. The twelfth-grade program concentrates on literary genres, art forms, and techniques. In a sense it is in this year of the program that the student brings together his earlier experiences with literature and makes generalizations (usually of his own) which equip him to deal with newer selections knowledgeably. To the new selection he simply applies what he has learned: he is able to see the kinds of manipulations which contemporary writers perform on established genres and art forms of literature. The tenth grade program is comprised largely of world literature in translation and thus exposes students to the earlier genres: myth, epic, tragedy, etc. American literature comprises the literary material of the eleventh grade and English literature of the twelfth grade. Though these kinds of literature are usually assigned to these three years, the manner in which the Carnegie curriculum asks teachers to present these materials is not traditional. For example, each of the published volumes of the three-year program emphasizes the importance of inductive teaching. Each represents the classroom as a place where students *discover* knowledge and skills, and not a place in which an authoritarian teacher dominates the scene and *tells* students what literature is. The volumes contain a good many recommendations and suggestions which help the teacher to understand his role as "neither preacher or lecturer, but guide, discussion leader, arbiter, and perhaps occasionally resource person." At first the teacher is asked to follow the lesson plans outlined in the teacher's edition of the volumes. Once he has worked his way through a course, he is then urged to be more flexible, particularly when he has mastered techniques which successfully involve students in discovery.

At the Oregon Curriculum Study Center the director and his associates decided to design an English curriculum for grades seven through twelve, which is also comprised of language, literature, and composition components. This program has a range with which all but the slowest can be accommodated in the study of English. The Oregon Center prepared an essay which explains its justification for changes in the English curriculum on three principal grounds: "First, textbooks, curriculum guides, and English teachers themselves have shown much uncertainty about the proper limits and purposes of English as a school subject"; second, "the existing curriculum shows a lack of sequence that has made order of learning difficult, some-times impossible"; finally "much of the material in the existing cur-riculum is out of date, reflecting little or no awareness of the present state of knowledge in such relevant disciplines as linguistics, semantics, rhetoric, literary analysis and criticism, and the psychology of learning."

After defining literature as a "record of the most thoughtful and perceptive men of all ages," the Oregon program delineates an ap-proach "predicated on the axiom that the study of literature is a discipline — that it is a study of value in and for itself, and that it has its own laws of operation and its own vocabulary." The Oregon pro-gram also places literature at the center of its curriculum concern and attempts to build a sequential, integrated literature program involv-ing three main components — subject, form, and point of view. These are treated simply enough so that young readers can understand them and yet so that none of the works are distorted to accommodate this framework of study. *Subject* suggests that "any work of literature is about something" — often on several levels — and asks "generaliza-tions from the reader" to help him discover that "a work means as well as tells." *Form*, "on all levels of literature, is a verbal and artistic structuring of ideas just as the thought in a sonnet must somehow be packed into fourteen lines of iambic pentameter." The Oregon litera-ture component subscribes to the idea that studying form will "result in the student's being aware of the arousal and satisfaction of expecta-tions. Although point of view is "traditionally taken to mean the angle of vision of the narrator," in this program it is enlarged to include "various attitudes toward the subject of the work — that of the author, that of the characters, and that of the reader." The Oregon Curriculum has attempted to build in it assurance that students will develop "the skill to understand any work of literature." Thus, the test of success for this curriculum would be the students' ability to apply the tools of understanding to a work outside the curriculum. Inherent in the program is the principle that the curriculum "will function inductive-ly." The Oregon program places literature at its center "on the grounds that it is at or near the center of humane studies . . . and in-forms our whole character."

The Nebraska Curriculum Development Center originally set out to prepare a sequential program in composition. It defined seven areas related to composition: (1) Composition and the usable portions of classical rhetoric; (2) composition and the possibility of a new rhetoric: the theoretical possibilities of "discourse analysis" and re-cent British studies of the philosophical "grammar and logic" of language; (3) composition and its relation to structural and trans-formational grammar; (4) composition and close reading: the teaching of literature and its use as a rhetorical or structural model; (5) the construction of criteria and tests for the measurement of excellence in composition; (6) the analysis of levels of student maturity at which basic composition "habits" or "patterns of decision" are formed; and (7) the construction of criteria and tests for the correction of themes in the areas of syntax, logic, and persuasive strategy.

The directors and their colleagues realized that a composition program cannot, by itself, be viable. It needs the contexts of literature and language if it is to have a chance of succeeding. They also real-ized that no program for grades seven to twelve would be practical, since elementary schools vary so much in their work with the language arts that a secondary-school program could not be built on a realistic basis. For this reason the Nebraska Center undertook to build the program for grades one through twelve and provided for the three components subscribed to by the Carnegie-Mellon and the Oregon programs by considering composition as growing out of the study of literature and language: literature-and-composition and language-and-composition.

The Nebraska Curriculum in respect to the literature component exhibits the belief that the study of literature should acquaint students with some of the best that has been thought and said in Western cul-ture. It believes that literary study should provide both an esthetic and a moral experience. It takes the stand that in order to understood contemporary culture we have to look at literary forms, ideas, and values of earlier cultures which have been influential in shaping our own.

The literature program is divided into units, especially in the secondary school, each of which is structured in this fashion: At first students are directed to read a series of short selections, to answer questions over them, and finally are expected to discover the concept central in the unit. Then students proceed to work with a core text, usually an extended work, and apply to this study the concept(s) which they have learned and which now form a tool, a literary, critical one, by means of which they can discover the structure and meaning of a particular literary selection. Then students may also be asked to work with a supplementary selection and, on their own, to apply to it the tool(s) which they have made their own and which will enable them to get at the supplementary work successfully.

Sequence is established in the program by beginning with a very simple selection and building on it through grades one through twelve by the use of increasingly complex selections which are concerned with the same genre, or theme, or value, or idea. By exposing students to the same element from three to six or seven times during grades one through twelve, the program creates both a sequence and a spiral which naturally becomes a part of the students' literary education and a set of tools which he ultimately uses spontaneously as he is introduced to, heretofore, to him unknown, literary selections.

The Nebraska Curriculum states that literature is an art form having its own stylistic devices and its own structures or forms. If students are to understand what a literary work has to say, they must learn the most important of these conventions. For example, stories tend to fall into a certain form within particular cultures, or into certain sets of forms, and to use certain conventions. The epics, the comedies, the tragedies of a particular culture tend to fall into patterns, to shift them, to make what may be called stylistic changes in these patterns. One of the main concerns of this curriculum is to describe these conventions of literary communication and to identify them with the cultures in which they arose. In grade seven two units, "The Making of Stories" and "The Meaning of Stories," and in grade nine one unit, "Attitude, Tone, and Perspective: The Literary Kinds" are specifically designed to formalize much of the teaching of these characteristics of literature which have occurred in the earlier grades.

The literature component of the Nebraska Curriculum leans heavily upon the theories of Northrop Frye. Although the literature component of grades one through six does not attempt to ask students to master literary terminology, it does acquaint them with literary form of an extremely simple sort. By acquainting young students with certain narrative patterns which children's stories display, the program prepares them for an easy understanding later of certain often-used literary structures. For example, in the first grade the reading of *Little Tim and the Brave Sea Captain* gives the student a basic, though elementary, understanding of the epic structure. When the student encounters other selections using the same structure in later grades, he is likely to make discoveries which give him insight into the manner in which writers structure their stories. Recognizing the characteristics of epic structure, for example, gives him the key with which to unlock the variations on the epic which he will encounter. For example, the student of the Nebraska Curriculum studies *Homer Price* in a fourth-grade unit, *The Wind in the Willows* in the sixth grade unit, *The Odyssey* in a ninth-grade unit, *The Adventures of Huckleberry Finn* in an eleventh-grade unit, and *Paradise Lost* in a twelfth-grade unit. There are other examples of the epic structure in units at other grade levels, but the foregoing should explain the nature of how sequence is built and the spiral established and how the characteristics of epic form ultimately become a part of the student's literary-critical tools.

In addition to the epic, the Nebraska Curriculum also established sequences displaying the characteristics of the myth, the fable, the romance, the comedy, and the satire. All of these begin early in the elementary school program; the tragedy, however, is not introduced until the student achieves the maturity of a tenth-grader.

The Nebraska Curriculum also builds sequence and spiraling in other primary aspects of literature: themes, values, and ideas which are basic to and unique with man. It also draws its literary examples from a variety of cultures, all of which are background to, and have been influential in shaping, contemporary American culture. For example, one theme which runs through humane letters is concerned with man's attitude toward nature. The Nebraska Curriculum uses *The Little Island* in the first grade to show nature as an oppressor of man, *Charlotte's Web* in the fourth grade to show death as a natural process. In the seventh grade the American Indian myth reveals nature as animistic; in the tenth grade *The Open Boat* displays the idea that nature operates according to inexorable laws in which the individual may be tragically caught, and also units in the seventh grade involving Thoreau and in the twelfth grade involving the Romantic poets which show nature as benevolent, as moral teacher, and as spiritual inspirer.

There are also units treating man and his relation to his society and man and his relationship to a supreme being. These sequences are as much concerned with the themes of Western culture as they are with the values and ideas which our literature displays.

For a person preparing to teach in the secondary school or even for an experienced teacher, any unit of the secondary-school program examined out of context may seem to be too challenging. Though this program was not designed for the academically deficient student, it is suitable for the average and better-than-average student. What the person who has not taught the program has to do is to get sufficiently acquainted with the total sequence of the program to see how foundations are firmly built in the elementary school and early junior high school years to undergird the more challenging units of grades nine through twelve. Teachers who have done this and students who have been taught for a sequence of three years find that the units of the Nebraska Curriculum are not too difficult for most secondary-school students to master. In fact, some students, bored with the immature

expectations of schools, have, for the first time, become enthusiastically involved in the study of literature when they have been introduced to the Nebraska Curriculum, and teachers engaged in studying
and teaching it have gained satisfaction from the learning which they
derive from the program and how to teach it well, and display that
confidence which we find characteristic of a truly informed and professional teacher.

However, the programs of Carnegie-Mellon, Oregon, and Nebraska are all highly structured ones. They are programs which the
British participants in the Dartmouth Conference rejected simply
because they seemed too restrictive to the teachers of a nation which
after a good many years was finally getting rid of English syllabi
equally complex in structure.

The Hunter College Gateway English program, unlike the programs previously described, is not for the average or better-than-
average student. Instead it is "a comprehensive literature and
language arts program aimed at involving disadvantaged urban
adolescents in meaningful reading experiences." It introduces selections "chosen because students have found them interesting and
especially relevant to the problems they themselves have to face."[1]
In this program literature serves to help students gain "emotional
independence and maturity" and to enunciate satisfying "personal
codes and values." This program, too, is structured inductively, em-
phasizing discovery rather than memorization and simple recall. *A
Family Is a Way of Feeling, Stories in Song and Verse, Who Am I?*,
and *Coping* comprise a year-long program for an estimated reading
level of fifth through seventh grade. The eighth and ninth grade programs are also designed to motivate students to learn and to discover
that school is about real things with genuine value for them. The
Gateway Curriculum makes use of recorded poems and songs, literary
selections of such recent poets as E. E. Cummings and Gwendolyn
Brooks. It is handsomely illustrated and has a manual for teachers
which states that the program is not meant "to serve as a rigid formula
which must be adhered to blindly." The three programs developed at
the centers described earlier in this chapter allow the teacher flexi-
bility in the use of these programs, similar to that recommended in
the Gateway series. Unlike the Nebraska Curriculum, Gateway does
not believe that the study of literature is for the purpose of acquiring
a body of knowledge about literature. Though this principle is not
dominant in the Nebraska Curriculum, it is present. Gateway instead
emphasizes that the students' honest involvement with the literary
experience is primary. Although this program was focused upon

urban disadvantaged youth, adolescents from many cultural and economic backgrounds have studied it enthusiastically. Although the Gateway Program does not attempt to cover more than a three-year range, it does provide an engaging program for those young people who may be contemplating dropping out of school. Its use may very well help to enhance the holding power of the school with a high percentage of economically and culturally disadvantaged young people.

The four programs described in this chapter are the most outstanding of those developed at the Office of Education supported English curriculum study centers. The reader who is interested in learning about the partial or the somewhat extensive programs developed at the other centers might write the National Council of Teachers of English, specifically ERIC (Educational Resources Information Center), for information about these. ERIC collects, catalogs, abstracts, indexes, reproduces, and disseminates the results of various kinds of educational research, and that concerned with research in English may be obtained from this center.

As a whole, the programs developed by the curriculum study centers financed by the Office of Education during the nineteen-sixties are the most impressive and have had the strongest impact upon English curriculum changes. It is for this reason that the work of four of these centers, particularly their literature component, has been explained in this chapter. Some further experiments in literature programs will be explained or referred to briefly in the final chapter of this book.

SELECTED READINGS ON UNDERSTANDING AND TEACHING LITERATURE

The following bibliography is not an exhaustive one. In spite of its length, all of the books listed with, perhaps, the exception of the final category, are first-rate books. The final category lists the best available but in this case one could want better ones. They have been grouped into categories, such as "background," "the hero," etc., so that the beginning teacher can find his way quickly to the titles of the books which he feels himself in need of. The category captions indicate with what subject each of the books is involved. Although this list might have been longer, the author sees no virtue in overwhelming the beginner with far more reading than he can possibly cope with.

Background Books

AUERBACH, ERIC. *Mimesis* (trans. Willard R. Trask). Princeton, New Jersey: Princeton University Press, 1953.

BETT, HENRY. *English Myths and Traditions.* London: B. T. Batsford, Ltd., 1952.

BROOKS, CLEANTH. *The Well-Wrought Urn.* London: D. Dobson, 1949.

BOWRA, C. M. *From Virgil to Milton.* London: St. Martin's Press, 1948.

EMPSON, WILLIAM. *Seven Types of Ambiguity.* London: Chatto and Windus, 1947.

FRYE, NORTHROP. *Anatomy of Criticism.* Princeton, New Jersey: Princeton University Press, 1957.

GAUTIER, LEON. *Chivalry.* London: George Routledge and Sons, 1891.

LEWIS, C. S. *The Allegory of Love.* London: Oxford Press, 1946.

LORD, ALBERT. *The Singer of Tales.* Harvard University Press, 1966.

TILLYARD, M. W. *The English Epic and Its Background.* London: Chatto and Windus, 1954.

WILLIAMS, GEORGE H. *Wilderness and Paradise in Christian Thought.* New York: 1962.

The Hero

CAMPBELL, JOSEPH. *The Hero with a Thousand Faces.* New York, 1956.

GUMMERE, FRANCIS B. *Beowulf: The Oldest English Epic.* New York: Macmillan, 1909.

HOOK, SIDNEY. *The Hero in History.* New York: Humanities Press, 1950.

MCNAMEE, MAURICE B. *Honor and the Epic Hero.* New York: Holt, Rinehart and Winston, Inc., 1960.

The Novel

BOOTH, WAYNE C. *The Rhetoric of Fiction.* Chicago: University of Chicago Press, 1961.

BROOKS, CLEANTH, and ROBERT PENN WARREN. *Modern Rhetoric,* 2nd edition. New York: Harcourt, Brace and Company, 1958.

———. *Understanding Fiction,* 2nd edition. New York: Appleton-Century-Crofts, 1959.

GORDON, CAROLINE, and ALLEN TATE. *The House of Fiction.* New York: Scribner's, 1960.

VAN GHENT, DOROTHY. *The English Novel: Form and Function.* New York: Holt, Rinehart and Winston, 1953, 1961.

Satire

ALTER, ROBERT. *Rogues's Progress: Studies in the Picaresque Novel.* Cambridge, Massachusetts: Harvard University Press, 1964.

ELLIOTT, ROBERT C. *The Power of Satire*. Princeton, New Jersey: Princeton University Press, 1960.
HIGHET, GILBERT. *The Anatomy of Satire*. Princeton, New Jersey: Princeton University Press, 1962.
KERNAN, ALVIN. *The Cankered Muse*. New Haven: Yale University Press, 1959.
LEWIS, R. W. B. *The Picaresque Saint*. Philadelphia: J. B. Lippincott, 1959.
MACK, MAYNARD. "The Muse of Satire," *Studies in the Literature of the Augustan Age,* ed. R. C. Boys. Ann Arbor, Michigan: George Wahr, Publishing Company, 1952.

Tragedy

ARNOT, PETER B. *Introduction to Greek Theatre*. Bloomington, Indiana: Indiana University Press.
BENTLEY, GERALD. *Shakespeare and His Theatre*. Lincoln: University of Nebraska Press. (Bison Book 179).
BROOKS, CLEANTH. *Tragic Themes in Western Literature*. New Haven: Yale University Press, 1955.
BOWRA, C. M. *Sophoclean Tragedy*. London: Oxford University Press, 1944.
GUTHRIE, W. K. *The Greek Philosophers*. Harper Torchbook (TB1008).
HALLIDAY, FRANK E. *Shakespeare and His Age*. New York: Tomas Yoseloff, Publisher, 1964.
KRUTCH, JOSEPH WOOD. *Tragedy: Plays, Theory, and Criticism*. New York: Harcourt, Brace and World, Inc., 1960.
FARNHAM, WILLARD. *The Medieval Heritage of Elizabethan Tragedy*. Berkeley: University of California Press, 1936.

Comedy

CORNFORD, F. M. *The Origin of Attic Comedy*. New York: Doubleday and Company. (Anchor A263).
KERNAN, ALVIN B. *Character and Conflict: An Introduction to Drama*. New York: Harcourt, Brace and World, Inc., 1963.
NORWOOD, GILBERT. *Greek Comedy*. Boston: J. W. Luce, 1932.

Poetry

BROOKS, CLEANTH, and ROBERT PENN WARREN. *Understanding Poetry*. New York: Henry Holt and Company, Inc., 1938.
DREW, ELIZABETH. *Discovering Poetry*. New York: W. W. Norton and Company, Inc., 1932.
_____. *Poetry: A Modern Guide to Its Understanding and Enjoyment*. New York: Dell Publishing Company, Inc., 1959.

GWYNN, F. L., R. W. CONDEE, and A. O. LEWIS, JR. *The Case for Poetry.* Englewood Cliffs, New Jersey: Prentice-Hall, 1965.
ROSENTHAL, M. I., and A. J. M. SMITH. *Exploring Poetry.* New York: Macmillan Company, 1955.

American Literature

BROOKS, VAN WYCK. *The Flowering of New England.* New York: Dutton, 1936.
DOWNER, ALAN R. *The American Theatre Today.* New York: Basic Books, Inc., 1967.
MATTHIESSEN, F. L. *American Renaissance.* London, Oxford University Press, 1941.
SPENCER, R. F., and JESSE D. JENNINGS. *The Native Americans.* Harper and Row, 1965.
STEWART, RANDALL. *American Literature and Christian Doctrine.* Baton Rouge, Louisiana: Louisiana University Press, 1958.

Teaching English

Board of Education, City of New York. *Teaching English for Higher Horizons.* New York: Board of Education, 110 Livingston Street, Brooklyn, New York.
BURTON, DWIGHT L. *Literature Study in the High Schools,* revised edition. Holt, Rinehart and Winston, Inc., 1964.
BURTON, DWIGHT L., and JOHN S. SIMMONS. *Teaching English in Today's High Schools.* Holt, Rinehart and Winston, Inc., 1965.
HOGAN, ROBERT F. (ed.). *The Range of English, NCTE Distinguished Lectures 1968.* Champaign, Illinois: NCTE, 1968.
HOOK, J. N. *The Teaching of High School English.* New York: The Ronald Press Company, 1959.
JENKINSON, EDWARD B., and JANE STOUDER HAWLEY. *Teaching Literature in Grades Seven Through Nine.* Bloomington, Indiana: Indiana University Press, 1967.
LOBAN, WALTER, MARGARET RYAN, and JAMES R. SQUIRE. *Teaching Language and Literature, Grades Seven-Twelve,* 2nd edition. Harcourt, Brace and World, Inc., 1969.
POOLEY, ROBERT C. (ed.). *Perspectives on English, Essays to Honor W. Wilbur Hatfield.* New York: Appleton-Century-Crofts, Inc., 1960.
SQUIRE, JAMES R., et al. *High School Departments of English: Their Organization, Administration, and Supervision.* Cooperative Research Project No. F 047. Champaign, Illinois: NCTE, 1964.
SQUIRE, JAMES R. (ed.). *A Common Purpose.* Champaign, Illinois: NCTE, 1965.

Walsh, Dorothy. *Literature and Knowledge.* Middletown, Connecticut: The Wesleyan University Press, 1969.
Weiss, M. Jerry. *An English Teacher's Reader, Grades 7 through 12.* New York, The Odyssey Press, Inc., 1962.

CHAPTER 4

New Developments in Language Curricula and Their Teaching

Jerome S. Bruner gave to the curriculum creators of the nineteen-sixties a psychological base for structuring any educational program. Northrop Frye applied this base to the structuring of literature and came up with a way that is as viable for the discipline of English as the ways that Bruner's base is for mathematics and the physical sciences curricula. The two theorists, Bruner and Frye, stand out; but when we consider the field of language and the changes which have transpired in describing and teaching our language in the past decade, we should be aware that instead of two there have been at least 20 outstanding grammarians who have contributed to defining the nature of language and informing us about it. We cannot consider so many in so short a book, but this chapter will refer to those earlier scholars of modern English whose research provided the base on which more recent scholars have built their particular systems. This chapter will also call attention to the several practical scholars who are responsible for the language component of school English programs, those who made its implications pedagogically useful.

For a good many years there was no English grammar as such; that is, no one had set down in writing the characteristics of the English language as spoken. But in 1762 Bishop Lowth prepared his *Short Introduction to English Grammar*, a prescriptive grammar which used the Latin grammar as a model into which it attempted to fit a Germanic-derived English. Because the English language, a word-order language, could not be made to fit into the Latin grammar apparatus, a highly inflected language, we got a great many exceptions to the rules which Lowth laid down. Lowth had presumed that the rules of modern English, like those of classical Latin, could be discovered and set down permanently. Thus the writer could look up the rules, follow them, and always be "correct." Modern scholars

36

of language know, of course, that our language changes; what one generation finds suspect another generation celebrates.

The usual definitions of the eight parts of speech are quite illogical. Nouns and verbs are classified according to meaning; pronouns, adjectives, adverbs, prepositions, and conjunctions according to function; and interjections according to their emotional intensity. The shift from meaning to function in defining pronouns, adjectives, adverbs, prepositions and conjunctions gives rise to certain bothersome ambiguities, since these categories tend to overlap. For example, an adjective is defined as a word that modifies a noun or pronoun and an adverb as a word that modifies a verb, adjective, or another adverb. Using these definitions, we can look at the following sentence to see why traditional grammar is often so inaccurate: "My sister's friend visited four European projects last spring." *Sister's* and *European* should be classified as adjectives and *spring* as an adverb. Logically then *my* and *last* must be adverbs because *my* modifies an adjective and *last* an adverb. Most grammarians, however, would call *my* a pronoun in the possessive case and *last* an adjective. Furthermore *sister's, European,* and *spring* qualify as nouns because they name persons or things.

These are only two examples of an available many which illustrate the inconsistency and ambiguity of traditional grammar. As the neophyte teacher becomes acquainted with structural and/or transformational grammar, he will see how much more accurate these ways of describing or explaining English grammar are. Both use the scientific method of observing and recording objective descriptions and of establishing verifiable generalizations about the language— both its nature and its functioning.

The Latinate English grammar dominated American schools for many years in spite of its obvious inadequacies which most students felt. Modern students in many instances respond well to the study of grammar which does not pose the multiplicity of exceptions which have always put off the American student seeking to master grammar.

With this background behind, we can now turn our attention to the "new grammar," as it is popularly called, and consider some of the scholars who contributed to its shaping. A student preparing to teach English in a secondary school should acquaint himself with both some of the earlier works on language and some of the later. For example, as early as 1921 Edward Sapir reported the results of his scholarly investigations which were opposed in several crucial respects to the traditional grammatical theory then being taught. In 1932 the NCTE published S. A. Leonard's *Current English Usage,* reported research which informed the academic world that there is little agreement among educated people respecting what is called "good" usage. One year later Leonard Bloomfield published his *Language,* which was among the very first efforts to describe the English language scientifically. In 1940 Charles Fries published the results of his research under the title, *American English Grammar.* This, too, was an attempt to describe American-English as it was used nationally and to suggest to schools what would constitute a workable program in the English language. His worked turned teachers' focus to the language that is actually used in conducting the major affairs of our country and away from the grammatical usages which have no validity outside the English classroom. His research made schools aware that the English curriculum should emphasize the tremendous range of resources which the English language offers the speaker, or writer, and should deemphasize the sort of "prune and prisms" attitude which English teachers for generations had been guilty of, an attitude going back to the age of Classicism in England and the age of formal rules. Finally, in 1947 George O. Curme published his *Principles and Practice of English Grammar.* This book represents English grammar not as a body of fixed rules but as a part of an evolutionary process, as "the stirring story of the struggles of the English-speaking people for a fuller expression of their unfolding life." And in this backward look we should not omit Henry Sweet's *New English Grammar,* which is also part of the foundation for change in the teaching of English grammar that occurred in the nineteen-sixties.

Traditional grammar textbooks for secondary schools tended to narrow the field of language study. The tendency in recent years on the part of language scholars and curriculum designers is to enlarge the scope of language study in the schools. In addition to the important considerations given to morphology, syntax, and phonology, the schools of the nineteen-seventies, which are on their toes, are also providing language activities which are concerned with the dialects of American-English; with matters of usage; with the historical development of the English language with special attention to its more recent history, from Anglo-Saxon to modern English; with semantics — how language means; with lexicography — the resources of the unabridged dictionary and the philosophical stance of dictionary-makers; and also with the manner in which grammatical considerations bear upon rhetorical ones. In the paragraphs which follow, we shall attempt to look at each of these aspects of language study very briefly in order that the reader may have some expectations of that with which he should be concerned when as an English teacher he undertakes to teach language.

Language study may be classified in three large categories: language form, language meaning, and language sound. Descriptive or structural linguistics is primarily concerned with form, both word form and sentence patterns; and with sound, the study of phonology. Generative or transformational grammar places its emphasis almost exclusively on form, not the morphology (word form) of the language but on the syntax (sentence patterns) of the language.

The "new grammar" does not emphasize skills; instead scholars believe that language study is a humane discipline and worthy in its own right to be included in the school English curriculum. Traditionally, textbooks and teachers have told students that they must learn their grammar so that they can compose. No research has ever been able to establish any important relationship between knowledge of grammar—especially is this true of traditional grammar—and the ability to compose, either orally or in writing. They held this view even in the face of the fact that when Shakespeare and Milton, two of our greatest writers, were writing their masterpieces, there was no English grammar existent in written form. Modern language scholars believe that the study of language has a built-in significant content which is worth mastering. Linguists define language as the oral language, point out that it is constantly changing, and say that change is normal. Furthermore, contemporary linguists do not discuss "correctness" in language use but "appropriateness," saying that all usage is relative to particular persons and situations. Linguists are also aware that the written language is a rather poor substitute for the spoken, since it is very difficult, and sometimes impossible, to represent in writing how the speaker stresses certain words, raises or lowers the pitch of his voice, or pauses or comes to complete stops in his oral discourse. Linguistics gives attention to these matters, which are called the supra-segmental features of the language.

Among the first to popularize structural linguistics and introduce it into English classrooms were Hall, Roberts, Postman, Gleason. These scholars wrote textbooks which could be used for a grade range of seven through thirteen. One of the most able and prolific popularizers of linguistics, Roberts was also among the first to introduce transformational grammar to the classroom by way of textbook. He converted to teaching materials for the classroom the theories of Noam Chomsky, who followed the structuralists with his theory of generative or transformational grammar. Though this grammar is somewhat more limited than structural grammar, it has had a more profound effect upon language scholars than has structural linguistics.

For the benefit of the neophyte or teacher uninformed about these two kinds of grammar, we will explain very briefly, and superficially, these two theories. We will begin with structural linguistics.

Morphology, a significant aspect of structural linguistics, is concerned with word forms alone and omits meaning considerations. For example, in the word *girlish, girl* and *ish* are two morphemes, the two parts which determine the meaning of the word. Because *girl* can stand alone as a separate morpheme, it is called a free morpheme, or word. Since *ish* does not stand alone, it is called a bound morpheme. It is bound to some other morpheme. Bound morphemes are also called affixes and may be attached to a free morpheme either at its beginning or at its end. For example, *dis* may be placed at the beginning of *enchant; ment* may be placed at its end. With these affixes we change the function of the root word. In structural linguistics we regard nouns as having four forms: singular *girl*, plural *girls*, singular possessive *girl's*, and possessive plural *girls'*. A noun, therefore, is a word which will take these three affixes: *'s, s, s'*; and it is not always the name of a person, place or thing. Nouns also have derivational suffixes, for example, *employ-ment* or *base-born*.

Verbs are characterized as words that will take the following affixes: (1) *s* (for third person singular); (2) *ed* (for past participle); (3) *ing* (for present participle). Adjectives are words which will take *er* and *est* as affixes or may be preceded by structure words such as *more* and *most*. Adverbs take *ly* as an affix. Pronouns are regarded as nouns, at least as noun replacers, and students are asked to look at some early English inflections which remain. For examples there are *my, mine,* and *me* derived from *I*. What are called articles, prepositions, and conjunctions in traditional grammar are here called noun determiners and structure words. They cannot be handled in any of the four form classes but serve to relate these form-class words in patterns which give meaning.

The form-class words are also identified by the slots into which they will fit in any utterance. For example, the noun slot may be between the noun determiner (article) and a verb or after a preposition or verb. Examples: The _____ ate. The day passed into _____. The automobile hit the _____. The verb slot is usually after a noun or preceding a noun or predicate adjective. Examples: The boy _____. We _____ lunch. The house _____ beautiful. The adjective usually precedes a noun and may also follow a noun determiner. Examples: _____ boys eat large portions. The _____ girl washed the dishes. The adverb is a movable which may come at the beginning, the middle, or at the end of most sentences. Examples: _____ the boys trudged to school. The boy trudged _____ to school. The boy trudged to school _____.

This explanation of structural linguistics is an extremely limited one. Its omission of a great many secondary matters will give rise to many questions which the young teacher will want answered. To get those answers, the teacher should investigate some of the books listed in the bibliography at the end of this chapter. The teacher might well begin with such simple textbooks as those written by Neil Postman or Paul Roberts.

Structural linguistics is also concerned with syntax. Some linguists believe that there are eight, others ten, basic sentence patterns. Using the following as a code, the reader will understand the formulas given below: N—noun, V—verb, Adj.—adjective, Adv.—adverb.

1. NV—intransitive (Adv.)	The boy breathed deeply.
2. NV—be (Adv.)	The boy is there.
3. NV—linking Adj.	The boy looked handsome.
4. NV—be Adj.	The boy is healthy.
5. NV—transitive N	The boy won the race.
6. NV—become N	The boy became the captain.
7. NV—be N	The boy is captain.
8. NV—give NN	The boy gave his teammates his medal.
9. NV—consider NN	The boy considered the race a challenge.
10. NV—elect NN	The boy elected his brother timekeeper.

Most structural linguists tend to divide the sentence patterns into two aspects, the noun phrase and the verb phrase, and then note how the other words in the sentence cluster around these two.

Beginning with kernel (a basic sentence pattern) sentences, students are taught how to add to these and to manipulate their elements into effective, harmonious, and interesting patterns. This approach to the study of the sentence is a positive one, since it teaches students how to combine a variety of elements into an interesting pattern. The parsing activity of traditional grammar worked in reverse: It taught students how to take apart interesting sentences, but this process impeded rather than increased students' composition skills.

The transformational grammarian believes that a satisfactory grammar of English should reveal how a native speaker of English understands what a particular sentence means even if he has never heard that sentence before or uttered a similar one. The scholar wonders how the human mind is able to sort out various sounds and arrange them into meaningful sentences. The transformationalist does build on the work of the structuralist, especially in phonology, but he goes further. He attempts to discover rules by which any possible sentence in English may be generated, whether or not it has ever been uttered. Phrase-structure rules explain how a variety of English phrases develop, and transformational rules describe the several arrangements and rearrangements of these phrases which may occur in the development of more complex and formally sophisticated sentences. *Phrase-structure rules* tend to reveal how sentences may be generated, and *transforms* tell us how to change present sentences or generate new ones.

To make this explanation clearer, let us see how a simple sentence can be generated and transformed. Let S equal sentence. Then S $\longrightarrow$ NP (noun phrase) plus VP (verb phrase), where $\longrightarrow$ indicates "rewrite as." This formula can stand as a model for a sentence we can now generate. The next step will be to rewrite NP by choosing a word like *house, automobile, driver*. The commas are here to indicate that we can choose only one word from the list. The fourth step is to choose one word from a second list which contains words such as *looks, swerved, guided* in order to rewrite VP. We now have generated a sentence such as "House looked new." or "The automobile swerved." or "The driver guided the vehicle." We could show the first sentence in a diagrammatic way, as in Figure 1.

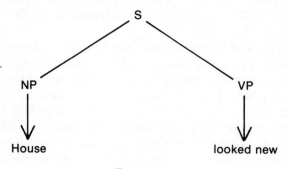

Figure 1

If we want to add determiners (articles) (D) or modifiers, our diagram would look like Figure 2.

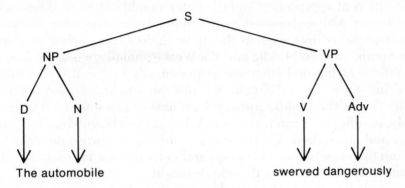

Figure 2

Simplifying the rules we can show how another kind of sentence can be transformed from the active to the passive voice. Take this pattern: $(D) + N + Vt + (D) + N$, which indicates that a determiner may introduce a noun which governs a transitive verb which takes an object introduced by a determiner. The sample sentence might be "The driver guided the vehicle." Now a passive voice sentence with the same total meaning can be generated by transforming the sentence in something like the following manner: 2nd N + be + V-en + (by + 1st N). The sentence produced reads "The vehicle was guided by the driver."

What should emerge from these explanations is the complexity of transformational grammar and its tendency to reduce language to formulas. These grammarians say that all sentences emerge from re-workings of simpler sentences. The transformationalists have also devised new diagrammatic ways of showing the surface and deep structure of a sentence, called tree diagrams, of which those in Figures 1 and 2 are very simple examples. Such kind of tree diagrams should help young people visualize the kinds of transformations, such as active to passive voice, which sentences are susceptible to, or else the young person should not be confused by being expected to master this approach to an understanding of syntactical patterns. Some young people do not have that kind of mind which makes it possible for them to see the trees in spite of the forest.

Phonology is treated by both structural and transformational linguists, the latter leaning upon the former. Phonology distinguishes approximately 35 different phonemes in English. (A phoneme is the smallest feature of the spoken language which differentiates what is said from what might have been said.) Phonemics and phonetics are two different approaches, and the latter should not be confused with the former. Although variations in pronunciation arise when one compares speakers from each of the major dialect areas—New England, the South, and the Middle and Far West—phonology teaches us how to represent the oral language graphemically by the use of a single spelling. One of our difficulties is that our spelling system is essentially that of the Middle Ages and has never been reformed, successfully, to reflect the extensive sound changes and borrowings that have occurred since then. Yet there is possibly more correspondence between the sounds of our language and our written representation of it than we have commonly thought or taught.

Students may also be introduced to phonology as a way of helping them to understand English prosody. The rhythm and rhyme patterns of poetry are more easily detected by the ear of a student given instruction in phonology than they are by the untrained. Phonological study is also an aid to the student when he uses punctuation. Hearing the junctures between sentence elements helps to train the writer in how to punctuate. The student with the untutored ear will not hear the pauses or, if he does, he is not so likely to be able to discriminate among them as finely as the student who has been trained to discriminate. The reader of this book will find the phonemic alphabet given in almost all linguistic books of a structural nature. He can quite easily teach himself that alphabet and how to transcribe his language by means of it.

The study of phonology leads very naturally to the study of dialectology. Dialectology is concerned with these variations in pronunciation and those variations in meaning of certain vocabulary items which obtain in the three major dialect areas of the United States: New England, the South, and the Midwest and Far West. Very young students need to be shown how colorful and interesting these variations are; the variations enhance the richness of the texture of American-English speech. Since a person who is illiterate in respect to dialectal variations often assumes a snobbish stance, believing his own dialect to be the preferred one and his neighbor's to be inferior, it is good that schools are clarifying the subject and eradicating this kind of snobbishness which divides rather than unites people. For example, here follow some pronunciation variations to illustrate common dialectal differences:

EASTERN NEW ENGLAND AND NEW YORK CITY		MIDDLE AND ATLANTIC	THE SOUTH
1. far	/fa/	/far/	
2. farm	/fam/	/farm/	
3. law	/lar/	/law/	/lo/
4. orange	/arɨndʒ/[1]	/orɨndʒ/[1]	
5. greasy		/grîysiy/	/griyziy/

And here follow some variations in vocabulary meanings in the three regions:

1. pail	bucket	bucket or slop bucket
2. burlap bag	gunny sack	croker (crocus) sack
3. skunk	skunk, polecat	polecat
4. spider	skillet	frying pan

The study of dialectology is also a good introduction to the study of usage. One of the reasons why American schools have failed to hold secondary-school students through to graduation is that too many teachers know almost nothing about dialects and how to regard the language variations to be found in many classrooms. Usage has to do with a matter of taste, the words which a speaker chooses to use in communicating. It also has to do with matters of appropriateness— what dialect one uses should be determined by the social situation and the nature of one's audience, formal or informal, literate or illiterate, public or intimate.

For many years teachers have believed that there is a standard English and that departures from standard English usage show a lack of education or breeding. It may be true that there is a body of English usages which educated people practice fairly well; yet when we undertake to establish what this body is, there is disagreement. (Charles Fries's research should have laid this controversy to rest 30 years ago.) Educated as well as uneducated have their individual dialects, and one is not inferior and the other superior. Mrs. Malaprop becomes an object of humor when we hear her attempts to emulate the speech of a lady high in London society and the Court. Teachers have also been concerned with "correctness" and "incorrectness" of usage. Since the United States has no academy, as does France, to rule on such matters, we cannot defend the position which too many of us teachers took for too long a time. It is as if the teacher were saying to the student: "I used to use the language incorrectly as you do now; but I overcame my bad usage. Now I have risen socially and expect to go higher because I am careful about my speech. And since I *made* it, I want to help you make it." But of course not all students are anxious to emulate what middle-class white teachers think is "correct" English. Actually we have to accept as appropriate the dialects which serve people in clear communication acts and in helping them hold to that bond which unites them. For example, teachers who make no attempt to understand the dialect of their black students and who try to teach these students that their dialect is inferior are themselves misguided and illiterate in this area of language. Not only do they fail to communicate with such students; they may also be the factor which causes black students to reach a decision to drop out of school. Teachers defend such attitudes toward black students by saying that these students must learn the white dialect if they are to get ahead economically. It has been the observation of a good many wise teachers that the black student does learn the white dialect and is able to switch to its use when he finds himself in a situation where it seems wise to switch. But because many black students continue to use their black dialect in the school environment, some white teachers think they are unable to use the white dialect. Too much tampering with their allegiance to their own dialect on the part of the white teacher may make the black students so uncomfortable that they lose faith in public education and withdraw from school. White teachers need to accept the black dialect in their classroom and to establish a rapport which will make school a comfortable experience for the black student. In fact, white teachers might go a step further. If they believe that black students should master their white dialect, should they not also be willing to master the main features of their black students' dialect?

A rather large body of material has been written during the past decade on usage matters, and young teachers should read some of these. A bibliography which contains the titles of books on usage has been placed at the end of this chapter. In addition, the beginning teacher might also find it profitable to subscribe to a bulletin which the Center for Applied Linguistics, 1717 Massachusetts Avenue, N.W., Washington, D.C., 20036, still publishes, *The Linguistic Reporter.*

Just as there has been much written about English usage, there is also a body of material on semantics, the meaning of words. We do not have the space to go into a detailed treatment of this subject, but a few facts should be stated. These facts represent a rather sharp break with the semantics theories popular earlier in the present century.

One milepost was reached in our growing understanding of this field when Merriam-Webster published their *Third International Dictionary of the English Language*. This dictionary grew out of linguistic scholarship and departed somewhat radically from the policies of earlier lexicographers. People in high positions but uninformed about linguistics attacked this publication because it failed to distinguish whether certain words currently enjoyed the status of standard English usage or were still considered colloquial. They also deplored its failure to continue its entries concerned with mythology and biography, features of the earlier dictionaries. Implicit in the attacks was the idea that dictionaries should be arbiters, whereas the editors maintained that they were only reporters on the state of the language.

We need to realize that word meaning is purely arbitrary. A word means only what meaning a community of speakers assign to it and not what it may have meant at an earlier time or place. And those semanticists that have tried to tell us that words are symbols of things in the real world have limited word meaning. We have many words in our language which have no referents in the real world. They derive their meaning from the context of the writing or speaking in which they appear. The young teacher should forget his Hayakawa and turn to Ludwig Wittgenstein[2] and the English philosophers[3] of language who have the most reliable information to give us about meaning.

Because the study of language has enlarged so much in the past decade, this chapter has become overlong. However, it is in this area that the neophyte or young teacher feels the most need for information. In spite of the length of this chapter, we should not close it until we have described very briefly the language curricula of the English curriculum study centers.

At Carnegie-Mellon the three-year language program is cumulative and moves from a study of the structure of the language, to semantics, to rhetoric (the effective use of language), and to the history of the language. The linguistic approach is structural rather than transformational-generative.

The Oregon Curriculum states that language should be taught because it is of such interest to human beings and is such an important part of their existence. Oregon uses the transformational-generative approach to the study of grammar. The center believes that "from a limited number of sentence types it is possible for native speakers of our language to recreate an infinite number of transformed sentences, sentences they have never heard or spoken." They reveal also how it is possible for native speakers of our language, by the time they are five or six years old, to understand most sentences they may come in contact with though they may never have heard the sentences before.

Grade seven of the Oregon language component is comprised of a sequence of rules known as phrase structure rules, which explain the grammatical utterances of English. These rules lead to a consideration of kernel sentences — simple, declarative, active sentences which are the primary sentences of the language. The program demonstrates that all other sentence types are generated from the kernels by processes called transformations. There is also a special unit which attempts to define various social levels of language.

Grade eight continues examining kernel sentences and their transformations, working with increasingly sophisticated processes. By grade nine the student is introduced to lexicography and the history of the language. The latter is taught again on a more sophisticated basis in grade twelve. The Oregon Center has also developed a series of useful films (distributed by McGraw-Hill, New York) in which Professor Wayne A. O'Neil explains the transformational process clearly. The films can be used best after students have worked through some transformational processes rather than as an introduction to the processes.

Like Oregon, the Nebraska Curriculum Study Center has prepared a very elaborate language program. It begins with the first grade. Children become involved in hearing stories or in reading them themselves, and then they are directed to certain features of the language displayed by the stories — vocabulary, rhythm, sound, form, etc. — by means of non-technical language. The language activities for the elementary school children are like games, interesting, challenging, and ultimately informative.[4] On this informal but rather wide-ranging language program, the language program of grades seven through ten is built. The language program for grades seven through ten is a structured one. It is concerned with language form — structural linguistics and some fairly simple transformational grammar are the approaches, with language meaning, and with language sound. A simple listing of the units here does not do justice to the program, but the interested reader can obtain copies for study. The listing will give a sense of the elaborateness of the program:

	GRAMMAR	MEANING	SOUND
Grade 7	The Dictionary	Form Classes (Morphology)	Phonology and Spelling
Grade 8	Words and Their Meaning	Syntax History of the Language	Phonology and Spelling

Grade 9	The Uses of Language Syntax and the Rhetoric of the Sentence	Syntax and Style: the Sentence[5] Dialects	Phonology
Grade 10	The Rhetoric of the Sentence[6]	Induction and the Whole Composition[6]	
Grade 11	The Rhetoric of the Paragraph[6]	The Meaning of the Whole Composition[6]	
Grade 12	Grammatical System and Conceptual Pattern[6] The Rhetoric of Longer Units of Composition[6]	Deduction and the Whole Composition[6]	

The Gateway materials developed at Hunter College have no formal language program. This is not to say that the program does nothing with language. When one considers the disadvantaged for whom this program is designed, it is evident why the program does not emphasize a formal body of information about language which junior high school students might be expected to master. The materials are literature-centered. Various aspects of language — form and structure of words and sentences, the meaning of certain vocabulary items, and especially matters of dialect and usage — are studied informally and in the context of literature. A three-year program such as this can give students, almost unconsciously, a good amount of information and can modify, for the better, their speaking, writing, and understanding. The program is noteworthy because it avoids the stigmatizing that often happens when a classroom of disadvantaged students collide with a middle-class teacher who denigrates their dialect and attempts to impose her own on them. The very nature of the literature should make the sensitive teacher — even if given no instruction — avoid so unpleasant and destructive a confrontation.

The curriculum study centers at the University of Minnesota and Northern Illinois University worked almost exclusively with the preparation of language materials. Although so far these have not become as accessible to teachers as the materials at the four other centers dealt with here, an interested teacher might try to obtain the materials by addressing the English department at either university.

The treatment here of language as a component of the English program is, at best, very incomplete. Volumes could be written and have been. The purpose of this chapter has been to alert the young teacher to the scope of this component, to arouse his interest in the new grammars, and to urge him to begin to inform himself.

SELECTED READINGS IN LINGUISTICS

Background Books in Linguistics (Pioneering Works)

AIKEN, JANET RANKIN. *A New Plan of English Grammar.* New York: Henry Holt and Company, 1933. A simplified and coherent functional approach but now out of print.

BLOOMFIELD, LEONARD. *Language.* New York: Holt, Rinehart and Winston, 1933. An early trailblazer in linguistics for those who have followed.

CURME, GEORGE O. *Syntax.* New York: D. C. Health, 1931. *Parts of Speech and Accidence.* New York: D. C. Health, 1935. A fully packed grammar, this is probably the best known of American grammars from an old-fashioned functional point of view.

FRIES, CHARLES CARPENTER. *American English Grammar.* New York: Appleton-Century, 1940. This makes no concessions to academe but reports the language as Americans write it.

————. *The Structure of English.* New York: Harcourt, Brace, 1952. The most influential study of spoken English; a well-written structural grammar.

JESPERSEN, OTTO. *Growth and Structure of the English Language.* Garden City, New York. Especially strong in showing language change, particulary English morphology.

LOWTH, ROBERT. *A Short Introduction to English Grammar.* London: 1762. This is an "Englished" Latin grammar with descriptive usage based on Latin and "logic" included; this book has influenced many of the grammar texts which followed.

PEDERSEN, HOLGER. *The Discovery of Language.* Bloomington: Indiana University Press, 1931. For its time this book was noteworthy because it taught us a new stance to take as we looked at language.

SAPIR, EDWARD. *Language: An Introduction to the Study of Speech.* New York: Harcourt, Brace and World, 1921. One of the earliest works to alert us to the necessity to describe language and to preserve in written form the languages which are dying out.

SAUSSURE, FERDINAND DE. *Course in General Linguistics.* New York: Philosophical Library, 1959. Saussure took linguistics from philology, where it had traditionally been, and associated it with anthropology.

STERN, GUSTAF. *Meaning and Change of Meaning.* Bloomington: Indiana University Press, 1931. A realistic approach to semantics which freed the subject from traditional, inaccurate ideas.

SWEET, HENRY. *New English Grammar*. 2 vols. Oxford: 1892, 1898. Perhaps the bravest attempt ever to present a logical grammar; it is also historical.

ZANDVOORT, ROBERT. *A Handbook of English Grammar*. London: Longmans, Green, 1957. A traditional grammar but defensible for its richness of detail.

Scholarly, Theoretical Books in Modern Linguistics

ANDERSON, WALLACE L., and NORMAN C. STAGEBERG (eds.). *Introductory Readings on Language*. New York: Holt, Rinehart and Winston, 1966. A variety of articles collected and valuable for the beginning student of linguistics.

BACH, EMMON. *An Introduction to Transformational Grammars*. New York: Holt, Rinehart & Winston, 1964. The author was ready to withdraw this book almost as soon as it was published; yet it is still an easier book for beginners than are Chomsky's books.

BLOOMFIELD, MORTON W., and LEONARD NEWMARK. *A Linguistic Introduction to the History of English*. New York: Alfred A. Knop, 1963. A presentation of the history of the English language as described from a scientific stance.

CHERRY, COLIN. *On Human Communication*. New York: John Wiley & Sons, 1961. Original insights into the nature of communication among human beings.

CHOMSKY, NOAM. *Syntactic Structures*. The Hague: Mouton and Company, 1957. *Cartesian Linguistics*. New York: Harper & Row, 1966. These two books introduced linguists to an original way of looking at language and determining the nature of grammar and have had, more than almost any other recent works, a profound and widespread effect on the subject and its practitioners.

DINNEEN, FRANCIS. *An Introduction to General Linguistics*. New York: Holt, Rinehart and Winston, 1967. A substantial treatment of a broad-range linguistics, more general than specific.

FODOR, JERRY A., and JERROLD J. KATZ (eds.). *The Structure of Language: Readings in the Philosophy of Language*. Englewood Cliffs, N.J.: Prentice-Hall, 1964. Useful in the same way as is the Anderson and Stageberg book.

HUDSPETH, ROBERT N., and DONALD F. STURDEVANT (eds.). *The World of Language*. New York: American Book Company, 1967. Useful in the same way as the Anderson and Stageberg and the Fodor and Katz collections.

IVES, SUMNER. *A Handbook for Writers*. New York: Knopf, 1960. This is a traditional grammar couched in traditional vocabulary.

LEHMANN, WINIFRED, P. *Historical Linguistics: An Introduction*. New York: Holt, Rinehart and Winston, 1962. A book similar to the Bloomfield-Newmark historical linguistics, one need not read both.

LENNEBERG, ERIC H. *Biological Foundations of Language.* New York: John
Wiley & Sons, 1967. This is an interesting examination of the child and
the manner in which he learns language and an examination of the biological basis for this potential.

LONG, RALPH B. *The Sentence and Its Parts.* Chicago: University of Chicago
Press, 1961. A description of the structures of standard American English,
a thorough treatment and attentive to the forms of the living language.

REIBEL, DAVID A., and SANFORD A. SCHANE (eds.). *Modern Studies in English.* Englewood Cliffs, New Jersey: Prentice-Hall, 1969. A respectable
collection of articles by a variety of language scholars.

SLEDD, JAMES. *A Short Introduction to English Grammar.* Chicago: Scott,
Foresman, 1959. A structural approach within the context of traditional
terminology, this book deals with phonology, morphology, and syntax,
and adds an excellent chapter on applied grammar, problems of English
prose style.

WATERMAN, JOHN T. *Perspectives in Linguistics.* Chicago, University of
Chicago Press, 1963. For its time a good report of the state of linguistics
and linguistic theory in the United States.

WHITEHALL, HAROLD. *Structural Essentials of English.* New York: Harcourt,
Brace, 1956. A structural description of the English language in individual terminology, a short book and exciting at the time of its publication.

WILSON, GRAHAM (ed.). *A Linguistics Reader.* New York: Harper & Row,
1967. Published more recently than other collections of similar nature,
it includes some new authors and their new ideas.

Textbooks and Popular Books in Linguistics

BROWN, DONA WORRALL, WALLACE C. BROWN, and DUDLEY BAILEY. *Form
in Modern English.* New York: Oxford, 1958. A structural approach in
traditional terminology useful in high school and college classrooms.

GLEASON, H. A. *An Introduction to Descriptive Linguistics.* New York: Holt,
Rinehart and Winston, 1961. It's clarity made this a popular textbook in
freshman college classrooms.

HALL, A. ROBERT, JR. *Linguistics and Your Language,* New York: Anchor
Book, Doubleday. Engagingly iconoclastic, this book was very popular
with the lay reader.

HOCKETT, CHARLES F. *A Course in Modern Linguistics.* New York: The Macmillan Co., 1958. Like the Brown, Brown, and Bailey and the Gleason
books, this became also a standard textbook in the nineteen-sixties before
the impact of Chomskian generative grammar took over.

NEWSOME, VERNA L. *Structural Grammar in the Classroom.* Milwaukee,
Wisconsin: Council of Teachers of English, 1961. This is a concise treatment of structural grammar, especially helpful to the classroom teacher
whose previous experience with linguistics is limited.

POSTMAN, NEIL, HAROLD MORINE, and GRETA MORINE. *Discovering Your Language.* New York: Holt, Rinehart and Winston, 1964. A clear and interesting book appealing to junior high school students, this was the first in a series of three which were used widely in the United States junior high schools at a time when teachers felt pressure to abandon the teaching of traditional grammar.

ROBERTS, PAUL. *Patterns of English.* New York: Harcourt, Brace, 1956. *Understanding English.* New York: Harper, 1958. The first a structural grammar for high school use and the second a full structural approach for college use, both books were extremely popular in the nineteen-sixties.

CHAPTER 5

New Developments in Composition Curricula and Their Teaching

The study of composition in the secondary school has been, at best, an experimental process. This has been true because almost no composition books written for the secondary-school classroom have been reliable. The fault has not been that of teachers. Too few have had any training in composition beyond the freshman composition courses offered by colleges and universities because few institutions of higher learning have offered such courses. Still fewer teachers have ever studied the classical, Renaissance, and later rhetorics. Teachers have in general accepted the textbooks which publishing companies have supplied them and have attempted to teach these books. That they were not successful in this effort they attributed more often to their own lack of skill than to the inadequacies of the textbooks. More discerning teachers, a minority, say that the textbooks did not work. These they put away and followed their own good sense in teaching young people how to compose.

The composition books for the secondary schools until very recent years have been a perpetuation of errors which earlier rhetoricians in English had made. As long as these rhetoricians adapted the larger structures of the ancient rhetoric to the English language, they succeeded fairly well. Paragraphs and total essays could be composed successfully within the formulas of ancient rhetoric. But when these same rhetoricians attempted to impose the rules of Greek (Aristotle) or Latin (Quintilian) on the Germanic-derived English language, they failed. The classical and Germanic languages are simply inimical to each other.

In spite of the fact that Richard Braddock[1] and others in 1963 made a careful examination of the most influential research that had been done in the United States in composition and found only three of a good number of such undertakings yielding any sizable amount of reliable information, a prominent Boston publisher as recently as 1964 brought out a series of unit lessons in composition which still echoed much of the early, questionable rhetoric and which, for a time, were widely used in classrooms.

Composition or rhetoric "is the discipline which should lead into effective ways of communicating, and students cannot find effective ways to communicate until they know they have choices; until they know what these choices are; and until they are encouraged to make choices in words, phrases, syntactic structures, ordering of material, modes of discourse, and the like."[2] This statement reflects the position to which a good many researchers had arrived by 1966 and suggests a point of departure for those who follow.

The linguists have been responsible for making students aware of the choices which the English language offers them as they pattern their ideas for communication purposes. Thus in the past decade those who would help develop a rhetoric within the boundaries of the English language have found the insights available through linguistics to be valuable. But before we look at the work of these rhetoricians, let us retreat momentarily and comment on a few earlier rhetoricians or works which have been influential.

In 1963 the National Council of Teachers of English republished a book first published in 1915 and written by Rollo Walter Brown. *How the French Boy Learns to Write* does exactly what the title indicates, Professor Brown's careful study of the techniques of a teacher of composition in a lycée. The usefulness of this book to the modern secondary-school teacher is summed up by Harold C. Martin in his "Foreword" to the 1963, NCTE edition. He says (p. vi): "It offers an exemplary attitude toward the teaching of the native language, an uncomplicated set of working principles, and enough verbatim reporting of classroom dialogue to make clear the way in which a teacher's learning and confidence free him to make the most of whatever line of inquiry opens up in class without for a minute losing direction or emphasis." The book functions as a reminder of what standards of excellence should be and can refresh the teacher as it provides him with valuable suggestions for teaching composition.

Another interim rhetorician whose theories bear directly on the nature of language meaning and anticipates the place of linguistics in rhetoric is I. A. Richards. And the work of Gilbert Ryle builds on Richards. The ideas of both should be useful to the neophyte teacher of English. Certainly a sound discipline in composition must be based on a working knowledge of grammar and an understanding of how language gets its meaning primarily in context.

With this background established, let us now look at some of the composition programs developed at the English curriculum study centers during the nineteen-sixties to see what ideas or materials might be useful and might help young teachers determine how they should begin when they would teach young people how to write.

At the Carnegie-Mellon Center the composition program for the senior high school was organized around the literary core of the program. More conventional than the Nebraska program, the composition program at Carnegie-Mellon begins with the selection of a general topic, narrowing that topic to manageable proportion in keeping with its purpose and audience, finding relevant data to support the topic, and finally modifying the message according to the needs or the expectations of the reader. The program provides for the development of proficiency in expository skills, the kind of writing which the high school student may be expected to succeed with at college. Although there are informal opportunities to work with "creative" writing—the composition of prose narratives and dramas, as well as poems—the major concern is exposition.

The Oregon Curriculum for grades seven though twelve characterizes the composing act as consisting of substance, structure, and style. "Substance is concerned with exploring in a responsible and even systematic way the world of facts and ideas which form the raw content of the act of communication. Structure is concerned with how to give organization and development to the substance chosen. Style deals with how to understand and use special, smaller quantities (word, phrase, and sentence) which will make composition better." The program believes that "drill, in the sense of merely repeating what others have written, can never lead students to the fundamentals of composing." The program goes on to say that "even the beginning writer must put things together—words, ideas, experiments, arguments—that have never been put together before." The composition program emphasizes what classical rhetoricians called "invention." The program stresses the development of habits of observation, discrimination, and imagination. In the Oregon Curriculum composition is both a writing and an oral act. Both a "usage manual," which permits a student "to answer many of his own questions on usage," and writing models, "samples of writing by professional writers which illustrate "the principles introduced in each grade," are contained in the composition component.

The Gateway Curriculum at the Hunter College Curriculum Study Center is an extremely informal one and, in view of the nature of the students who are and will be taught from it, it is informal in respect to composition. It recognizes that the act of writing is far more challenging to the disadvantaged students than is speaking. It places a premium on the students' learning to express themselves directly, avoiding the circumlocutions and redundancies so common among the unskilled. It also emphasizes the importance of honesty in speaking or writing. Since the literary materials of the program are exemplary for their directness and honesty, these two qualities are ever-present as students work with composition. Finally, the program is ready to wait until the student has a genuine desire to communicate his ideas. Here, again, the literary context is calculated to stir and arouse the students, to make them want to express their positions or share their experiences with others. Literature is here for itself but also for its effective quality. Speaking or writing becomes for some disadvantaged students a kind of psychotherapy. Though this program does not enunciate this as one of its principles, it is a valuable by-product for many disadvantaged students.

The Northwestern Curriculum Study Center concentrated primarily on the composition component of the English curriculum. In its program for grades seven through twelve it challenged popular methods of teaching students to compose and questioned the rationale which lies behind the composition textbooks, workbooks, and handbooks which have been most widely used in American secondary schools. In its introductory essay, the Northwestern Curriculum asks probing questions about the process of composing, examines the popularity with which some of the usable portions of the classical rhetoric were being used in secondary-school programs after several generations of use of a watered down, classically derived rhetoric, and urges students to experiment with language and to have confidence in their dialect.

One thing of particular value in the Northwestern composition materials is the exhibition of how foolish it is for English teachers to assign composition tasks to students mainly as a means of discovering their skill-level of usage and their deficiences in mechanics — punctuation, spelling, capitalization, etc. Another valuable aspect of the program was to make clear that composition in the secondary school should never be enslaved by a pretentious display of language or a refusal to look beyond words to facts. The program attempts to help students discover that writing itself can be "natural and pleasurable, the occasion and means of a satisfying (even a self-consummatory) experience instead of, as they too often still are, a chance for teaching that mysterious entity known as 'good' English."

The program also urges that a student be let "alone to do his own experimenting with his own grammatical and stylistic patterns and transformations." The program encourages students to include in their writing some of the lively accurate words, the complicated grammatical structures, and the relatively mature sentence patterns that they regularly use in their speech.

Though the Northwestern Curriculum materials outline nine steps which are to be followed and which teachers are likely to find helpful, it is probably more valuable for its function of disabusing teachers of the idea that they are more proofreaders than inspirers of creativity and for the contribution it makes in helping teachers to gain a sensible understanding of the value of each student's dialect and the necessity of the teacher's creating as natural an environment as a classroom can have in freeing young people to write. The Northwestern *Lessons in Composition* emphasize the process of writing rather than the completed product. These lessons are not so much concerned with "correctness" and the mastery of formal rhetorical devices as they are with personal and more creative writing.

The most elaborate composition program of the English curriculum study centers is the one developed at the University of Nebraska. This program is structured on literary models for grades one through six and also in part for grades seven through nine. In addition to much experimental work with language sound in the composing of verse, grades one through six students study a variety of children's stories and unconsciously absorb a sense of structure from the four or five basic motifs upon which all children's stories are structured.[3] In their cognitive development elementary-school children are not capable of argumentative or expository writing, but they can tell stories. So narrative writing constitutes the substance of the composition program for elementary-school children.

In grades seven through nine students have the opportunity to try out models other than the narrative. They may begin to do some rather loose persuasive or expository writing. They may imitate the dialog of drama, or try their hand at a variety of minor verse forms: haiku, limerick, ballad. They are allowed considerable freedom in the ways they may structure their written communication.

As we pointed out in the first paragraph of this chapter, linguistics brought to rhetoricians some valuable tools which might be put to work in the preparation of composition materials and in the teaching of composition. The Nebraska Program makes use of these tools in the preparation of its composition program. For example, it is in grade nine that students are introduced to their first formal rhetoric unit.

"Syntax and the Rhetoric of the Sentence" is derived primarily from the ideas of Professor Andrew Schiller, University of Illinois, Chicago Circle. This unit asks that the student have a firm ground in the eighth-grade unit titled simply "Syntax." The study of this unit helps students to see how many choices which the full repertoire of syntax offers them in composing. They have opportunities to see why they must make certain kinds of decisions in the sentences which they write. They need to be aware that the kind of speakers they assume themselves to be, the kind of subject with which they are dealing in their compositions, and the kinds of audiences to whom they are addressing their thoughts are all crucial factors in helping them to make the right decisions and choices. It is here in this unit that students move from simple, grammatical theory and practice into conscious, studied, rhetorical design. The four objectives of the unit are as follows: (1) to introduce the rhetorical possibilities of the sentence; (2) to inculcate the principle of revision in good writing; (3) to suggest what to look for in revising writing; and (4) to demonstrate and give practice on some techniques of revision.[4]

When we consider the rhetorical possibilities of the sentence, we recognize that in composing students have to make choices: They may choose active or passive voice, use declarative or interrogative, convert past tense to present; or they may interchange word for phrase or clause, phrase for word or clause, or clause for word or phrase. There is also the choice of location. Where in the sentence will the student place certain words and/or phrases. The slots for many are obligatory, but for others they are a matter of choice or taste. The student needs to be taught how to make appropriate choices. Another rhetorical concern may be how to pare a sentence and make it lean and muscular—to eliminate any redundancies. And a fourth, the counterpoint of the preceding, is how to expand a sentence, giving it body without eliminating its muscularity. In reality these are four ways of revising sentences,[5] and these kinds of revision are a part of rhetoric.

One of the most ingenious of the rhetoricians of the nineteen-sixties was Professor Francis Christensen, University of Southern California, and, at the time of his death, Northern Illinois University. Two rhetoric units of the Nebraska Curriculum, one on the sentence and the other on the paragraph, are derived from his theories. After each of these units was prepared by Professor Christensen, each was rewritten by teachers to shape each for the audience to which it was addressed, one for the tenth grade and the other for the eleventh grade. And after the revisions by teachers, both units also underwent further editing preceding their publication.

The first of these units, titled "The Rhetoric of the Shorter Units of the Composition: the Sentence" deals with the descriptive-narrative sentence. The rhetorical theories advanced in this unit are based upon the careful analysis which Professor Christensen made of hundreds of sentences written by 20 or more of the best contemporary writers. Professor Christensen discovered that most of the rhetorical principles of the sentence as expressed by classical rhetoricians are simply not true for the English sentence. For example, he discovered that 75 percent of the sentences written by recognized contemporary writers begin with a subject-predicate main clause. Fewer than 23 percent of the sentences of modern writers begin with adverbial clauses, and fewer than 1 percent of such sentences begin with a participle phrase. Thus the admonition of several generations of writers of language-composition textbooks to the reader to vary sentence openers is not valid. What Professor Christensen did discover is that the main clause is the least interesting part of the sentence. It is what we add as modifiers, especially after the predicate, which give sentences their interest and particularity. When we add modifiers before the noun, the modification moves forward; when we add them after the noun, the modification moves backward. The movement of the modern descriptive-narrative sentence is therefore in two directions, both linear. Since most modern sentences begin with a main clause, modifiers such as phrases and clauses usually follow. The main clause of the sentence is always general. To get specificity we must look to the modifiers which are added. And it is these additions which give interest to the sentence. Professor Christensen calls attention to the layers which are to be found in sentences, the layer aspect of sentences being well illustrated by Paul Robert's immediate-constituent principle.[6] Applied to modern sentences, this principle, according to Professor Christensen, displays the two-level and multi-level characteristics of such sentences. Perhaps we can make Professor Christensen's theories clear by using a sentence or two with which to illustrate.

For example, let us look at this sentence:

1. "Sometimes I lay,
    2. the sharp bones of my hips meeting only the hardness of the sand,
    2. the sun puckering my skin." (Nadine Gordimer)

The main clause here tells us almost nothing, has little of interest in it. But the subordinate elements which follow it, the two of equal

degree of specificity, add the real interest to the sentence. The main
clause is the generalization; the subelements are more specific.
Furthermore, the main clause tends to be abstract, while the subelements are concrete.

The same rhetorical principle may be seen at work in more
elaborate sentences, sentences with more than two levels. The following is an example:

> 1. "She sat surrounded by packages,
> 2. an orchid pinned to her dress above her left shoulder,
> 3. the petals fluttering with her movements."

In this sentence we find three levels. The second element of this
sentence modifies the first, the third modifies the second. In this sentence we move from generality to a second level and then again to a
third level of specificity. Modification in this sentence moves backward, the second element to the first, the third to the second. Professor Christensen[7] demonstrates this principle of rhetoric with far more
elaborate sentences in which there may be five or more levels, each
level growing more specific and concrete as it moves away from the
main-clause generality and abstractness.

Professor Christensen calls attention particularly to the widespread use which good writers make of certain constructions, both
noun and verb clusters as modifiers, but more especially of appositive
and absolute structures as replacers. These tend to pack into a very
few words some rather valuable information that sophisticates both
meaning and style. Although on the surface this may appear to be a
somewhat mechanical exercise, one should not underrate it. In the
first place, it gives students a useful tool with which they can create
far more interesting sentences, the kinds of sentences which professional writers create. In the second place, it reflects almost the first
serious inquiry anyone has made in attempting to determine what it
is that professional writers do and why their writing contrasts sharply
with the writing of amateurs. Instead of falling into the traditional
pattern of other rhetoricians and trying to keep alive a tradition which
has never been relevant to writers working in a Germanic language,
Professor Christensen has dared to analyze the sentences of many
writers, and he has had as a tool to serve him the information which
linguists have contributed to the field recently. Students who catch
the spirit of the principle of sentence composition which this unit
displays and practice it discover that their sentences have greater
density of texture and complexity of structure. Surprisingly, these

students commit fewer indiscretions of parallelism than do those who have never heard of the immediate-constituent theories of Paul Roberts.

In the Nebraska Curriculum the first unit in composition of the eleventh grade is titled "The Rhetoric of the Shorter Units of the Composition: The Paragraph." This unit was also written by Professor Christensen, rewritten by eleventh-grade teachers who used the original version in their classrooms, and given a still further editing preliminary to publication. This unit applies to the paragraph the principles which we explained Professor Christensen applied to the sentence. Here, however, one looks at the sentences not individually but as they appear in paragraph context. A paragraph often opens with a general statement. Then the sentence which follows the first usually reflects more specificity; the second may display the same level of specificity or it may move toward even more specificity. Some paragraphs are comprised of a series of sentences each showing greater specificity than the one preceding it. Using numbers, the lowest to illustrate the most general kind of clause, we can illustrate a variety of paragraph structures in this manner:

1.		1.		1.	
2.		2.		2.	
3.	OR	2.	OR		3.
4.		2.			3.
5.		2.		2.	
		2.			3.
					3.

Or almost any combination will serve to illustrate the variety of levels of specificity of which paragraphs are composed.

Professor Christensen's work with the sentence is with the descriptive-narrative sentence. His work with the paragraph is the expository paragraph. He believes that in descriptive-narrative writing the paragraph has little significance; that it is merely a grouping of sentences, a kind of convention which writers honor, the placing of smaller units into greater ones. But in expository writing he finds two kinds of paragraphs. One kind is like bricks or stones that constitute a wall, but the other is like mortar that holds the bricks and stones together. The second kind is generally short, consisting of introductions, transitions, and sometimes summaries and conclusions. The other kind is generally longer, especially in serious writing: it constitutes the substance of a piece of writing. It is with these two kinds of paragraphs that this rhetoric unit is concerned.

The second unit of the tenth grade in the Nebraska Curriculum is titled "Induction and the Total Composition." As the title suggests, this unit teaches students how to prepare a composition which calls for the proper assembling of a series of paragraphs. It is concerned primarily with argumentative-expository writing, that is, the academic dialect of writing. It is concerned to solve two frequent student problems in mastering this "dialect": finding something to say and getting it said in a fairly orderly way. The Nebraska Curriculum Center has found that the rhetorical theories of Aristotle and Quintilian are still useful in respect to the composition comprised of several paragraphs, and these theories have been adapted to the tenth-grader's use. *Invention* and *discovery* of classical rhetoric are particularly useful. However, this unit adapts or derives these — does not adopt either in their original entirety.

The teacher's manual for this unit gives a rather complete explanation of classical rhetorical theory and how to teach its useful parts. The student manual is comprised primarily of two major divisions. The first is concerned with *invention*. Here there is a structured series of 45 sets of questions which build the student's sense of what kinds of questions are relevant and necessary to given kinds of subjects and topics. The unit also gives an introduction to induction as it relates to composition. The second part of the unit focuses on *arrangement*. Here the unit displays models of strategies which professional writers use (a) to begin, (b) to summarize, (c) to refute, (d) to conclude essays. The purpose of these models is to lead the student to what conditions determine the selection of each kind of strategy. Then the unit deals with that aspect of classical rhetoric called *Elecutio.* However, instead of using Aristotle's rules of rhetoric for the word and sentence — useless since he was talking about the Greek rather than the English language — the unit refers back to Professor Christensen's theories of the rhetoric of the sentence and to the earlier units, the eighth-grade Unit 87, "Words and Their Meaning", and the ninth-grade Unit 95, "The Uses of Language." This section of the unit is here as a means of teaching the student a little about style. Both of these units are generated from the theories of language for which the English school of contemporary philosophy is known, the philosophy of such men as Ogden, Richards, Ryle, and Austin.

The second rhetoric unit of the eleventh grade is titled "The Meaning of the Total Composition: Ambiguities, Analogies, Contraries." The major concern of this unit is how people employ words to think. The unit provides students with the kinds of questions which they should raise about their own writing and the writing of others. These questions are both about words (and their uses) and *situations,* the contexts in which these words come into play and lead rather than mislead the reader.

The unit takes the students through a series of situations in which ordinary, and sometimes extraordinary, language is used. It gives them experience in determining whether various writers use language as they intend to use it, or whether they misuse it and in what ways. These exercises tend to teach the students how to control their language with a self-consciousness and clarity which they may never heretofore have had.

The unit is not concerned so much with the sentence as it is with a series of paragraphs. It looks at the uses of language in somewhat elaborate contexts to determine whether the author has control over his language or whether his language gets out of control.

The unit makes students aware of ambiguities — in which language may suggest meanings which are not in agreement; aware of analogies — in which the language employed in a certain context may be employed effectively in another but analogous situation; and finally how language employed in a particular context may be oppositely employed in a context which is directly contrary to the first.

The unit is very original. If it is well taught, students will become exceedingly conscious of the manner in which they use language and both analytical and critical of how responsibly and exactly they use it.

To understand how to teach the unit, the teacher has to get away from the Hayakawa[8] principles of semantics — where every symbol has a referent in the objective world — and into the English philosophic school in which context and situation alone determine the meaning of language. This is the world of Ludwig Wittgenstein, Gilbert Ryle, and J. L. Austin, a reality which can be known only through the language with which it can be described or explained.

Self-appointed critics who have not taught a unit such as this have claimed that it is too difficult for high-school students, but Nebraska teachers (and others) who have taught it to students who have studied the Nebraska English Curriculum from grade seven through ten have expressed satisfaction with their success in teaching it. The twelfth-grade program in composition, however, may be too challenging, particularly the second composition unit of the final year, "Deduction and Induction."

In grade twelve, the first composition unit, titled "Grammatical System and Conceptual Pattern: The Rhetoric of Paragraphs and Longer Units" attempts to teach students how to determine the difference between dependent and independent sentences, to see how certain syntactical structures signal specific kinds of relationships between sentence and sentence, to see how a series of sentences may be related to a single sentence in the total paragraph or to each other. This unit explores the use of symmetry and asymmetry in paragraphs, transpositions on the syntactic system for rhetorical effect, the self-conscious exploitation of the resources of grammar. In addition to the syntax sequence, this rhetoric unit also treats lexicon and rhythm and their contributions to the structuring of a rhetorical piece. Although only incidental here, the considerations of rhythm might be considered as belonging to the phonological or sound sequence of the language program of grades seven through twelve.

The second rhetoric unit of grade twelve is titled "Deduction and Induction." It attempts to involve students in a study of logic as logic is represented by language. The unit is divided into two parts: Part I deals with techniques for appraising deductive arguments, and Part II deals with techniques for appraising inductive arguments. This unit gives students a system for looking at the connections between statements and then asks students to observe them in the writing of their own essays and in their analysis of the essays of other writers, both amateur and professional. Before students can know whether the connections are right, they must be clear about what the statements are saying and what they mean within their context.

This unit is structured on both Aristotelian and modern symbolic logic. By involving students with increasingly more mature exercises in which the several facets of each system of reasoning, deductive and inductive, are used, the unit tends to make students more critical and thoughtful readers and more conscientious and responsible writers.

These seven rhetoric units, spread over grades nine through twelve, then, comprise the total rhetoric program of the Nebraska English Curriculum. In contrast to it, there is a very diversified, informal rhetoric program, especially that which is directly related to and growing out of the literature program. This part of the program gives students many opportunities to write and increases their facility in working with the written language. The varied exercises of the informal program also increase the students' ability to perform more skillfully as they become involved in the formal rhetoric program and its exercises.

This total rhetoric program has come out of a context in which all of the principles of earlier authorities so-called have been reexamined and, in doubtful cases, tested. If this program seems a radical one, it is radical in the sense that it makes use only of those features of the ancient rhetoric which are still useful and it makes use of modern linguistic theory as a means of making rhetorical analysis both possible and sensible. It also takes advantage of the new insights which the English philosophical school has contributed to the scholar interested in how language may serve his expressive needs and *how* it means.

At the present, with the exception of the Christensen program, there has not emerged a series of publications by professional publishers which purport to teach a rhetoric embodying the new insights which rhetoricians gained during the nineteen-sixties. The Nebraska English Curriculum on composition is useful; yet a beginning teacher need not think that he must adopt one of the very few composition programs. An experimentally minded teacher should read widely, of course, in rhetoric and composition to gain as much insight as possible in respect to the nature of this component of English and the manner in which it has been structured by various scholars and taught by various teachers in the past. The beginning teacher might develop an adequate composition program simply by allowing students to use their oral dialect in writing and by helping them to examine and analyze various written materials, especially literature, which can provide them well with models for their own writing. Since contemporary professional writers use the structures which earlier writers invented and manipulate these structures to make them suitable to their voices and to the substance of what they want to communicate, no teacher should be apologetic if he has his students try the same kind of strategies. Parody, for example, is attractive to young writers, and one who would like to use parody as a means of communicating his attitude and purpose in a piece of writing would need to become exceedingly familiar with parody generally, particularly its historical evolution, and also with the subject or the writing upon which he will base his original parody. Such attention means that the students writing a parody need to notice as many of the details of the original as they can discover so that their imitation will carry an entertaining similitude to the original.

One caution may be necessary. Inexperienced teachers should decide at the outset whether they are opting for "correctness" in students' writing or for honesty. This is not to say that spelling and other details of a composition would be overlooked. The teacher should just make sure that he looks first at what students feel it is important to say and whether they have expressed their ideas directly and honestly. Improving the accuracy of expression should be secondary, and the mechanics of written expression of still less importance.

An inexperienced teacher is sometimes criticized by a community which places a high priority on students' accuracy in written expression. If a teacher fails to penalize students for misspelled words, the community often tends to penalize the teacher. Teachers of English should pose questions to school patrons who think accuracy is foremost. Such questions should force patrons to make choices between the importance of substance and of form. Cleverly framed questions can cause the patron to see for himself which is the more important and influence him to cease his fault-finding. The teacher should steel himself against community intimidation which would keep him from performing the function for which he is best prepared: to teach understanding — and hopefully appreciation — of literature, to interest young people in discovering the major features of their language, and to impel young people to want to express in writing some of the feelings and ideas which excite them most. If correct spelling and attention to other mechanical details of writing should parallel the high quality of the young person's written ideas, then the teacher finds himself in a happy situation where he may be able to go ahead with his students at a more rapid pace than is usual.

Teachers should also provide students with opportunities to develop their oral composition skills. Informal kinds of oral composition tend to increase the quality of students' written composition. The more experience we have in shaping our communications, the more gracefully and economically we pattern them.

At one time in the profession there was a great stir about a theme-a-week. Many thought that this requirement would markedly improve the students' composition skills. Continuous writing will help give a student facility and exactness in his written expression, but little worthy writing can be done on the basis of a theme-a-week. For one thing, almost no teacher would have the energy or time to read a theme each week for all of his students. Secondary-school teachers of English are responsible for 75 to 180 students daily. Encouraging students to keep journals in which they write every day, one sentence to several paragraphs, does give students valuable experience. If the teacher can read in these journals from time to time, motivation is increased. The journal creates a more relaxed writing situation for both student and teacher and it makes writing a more manageable activity.

When it comes to assigning more formal writing, there are several things which the beginning teacher should remember. First, he should make sure that the students are provided, often by means of literary study, with an environment which makes them want to write. Moral problems posed in literature often excite a controversial response in the classroom. Giving each student a chance to express his views when controversy arises also gives him a reason for wanting to write and the opportunity to do some solid thinking to support the view which he takes.

Before the students begin to write, the teacher should help them explore possible ways by which they might structure their ideas most effectively. Also, the teacher should try to anticipate the kinds of difficulties that student writers will encounter. One percent of pre-vision is worth 99 percent of revision. In other words, it is seldom that a teacher should make a writing assignment on the spur of the moment. Almost always the writing assignment calls for a number of important considerations. If these preliminaries are taken into con-sideration, the teacher is likely to get more satisfactory writing from his students.

In the actual composition act, students may be put into groups of three to five to discuss their ideas with each other before they write. They may discuss what would be the best ways to structure the ideas which they want to communicate. Students can be taught to read and evaluate each others' written compositions and to suggest ways of improving. Finally, students can also learn to make a final evaluation of each others' writing. They are as quick to catch dishonesty in a colleague's writing as is the teacher, and the student will take such evaluation from his peers with better grace, often, than he will take it from his teacher.

In evaluating student writing, both teacher and students should try to answer questions such as these as they are addressed to a par-ticular manuscript:

1. What kind of structure is the writer using? How appropriate is this structure to what appears to be his purpose in this paper?
2. What is this manuscript seeking to do? How well does it suc-ceed? What interferes with its success? What contributes to its success?
3. Is the writer writing out of a genuine or an honestly imagined experience? What evidence in the paper do you find to support your answer?
4. Is the writer being honest — with his reader and with himself?

There may be other significant questions, but evaluation should not become cumbersome by including too many. The foregoing are likely to elicit the kinds of judgments which young writers will accept.

Some scholars believe that the ability to compose is born in a per-son and can never be taught. These same scholars believe that some few human beings are never able to develop composition skills comparable to their stage of maturity. Such beliefs may be true, but until we give students the opportunity to write and use our ingenuity to help them understand the ways that their compositions can be improved, we should not abandon hope for our students who have difficulty at first with composition. There is too much evidence available among students for the teacher to accept the idea that some students will never be able to compose with any degree of grace or effectiveness.

In the nineteen-seventies composition continues to pose questions. Scholars and teachers continue to experiment with techniques which they hope will help students write acceptably, if not well. Various diagrams or transparencies for the overhead projector have been created for the purpose of helping students organize their thoughts. There are film strips depicting various composition strategies. Some schools are experimenting with dictaphones or tape recorders, having students compose orally first and then convert, with revision, what they have dictated to written form. It is likely that teachers and schools will continue to theorize and experiment with the teaching of composition. For example, in a recent *English Journal*,[9] we find the following articles: "Saul Steinberg and High School Composition" by Lavonne Mueller; "To Sing the Street: Using a Community Film Program to Teach Composition" by Helen Foley; "Do Thirteen-Year-Olds Write as Well as Seventeen-Year-Olds?" by Henry B. Slotnick; "Implications of National Assessment Writing Results" by Edmund J. Farrell; "Film Stimuli—An Approach to Creative Writing" by Philip Dauterman and Robert Stahl. These constitute about a third of the articles in this particular issue and suggest that composition teaching will continue to puzzle teachers and to stimulate experimentation; and this is the manner by means of which, very slowly, new insights are gained and writing improvement grows.

To illustrate how much we still need to know about composition, we end this chapter with a listing of the questions which *Research in Written Composition* (Richard Braddock *et al.*) indicates remained to be answered at the time this book was printed:

Unexplored Territory

Some questions which seem fundamental in the teaching and learning of written composition apparently have gone almost untouched by careful research. This chapter concludes with a list of questions, not considered previously in this chapter, which indicate areas in which future investigators may wish to direct their efforts:

1. What kinds of situations and assignments at various levels of schooling stimulate a desire to write well?

2. What do different kinds of students prefer to write about when relieved of the expectations and requirements of teachers and others?
3. What are the sources of fear and resentment of writing?
4. How do the kinds of writing which adults compose vary with their occupations and other factors?
5. What is the effect on writing of having the student compose his paper for different kinds of readers?
6. At which levels of maturation does it seem appropriate to introduce the various modes of discourse — narration, poetry, drama, exposition, argument, and criticism?
7. What is the relative effectiveness of writing shorter and longer papers at various levels of maturity and proficiency?
8. At which levels of maturation does it seem appropriate to introduce the various rhetorical elements of writing?
9. What are the effects of various kinds and amounts of reading on the quality and kinds of writing a person does?
10. What are the direct and indirect effects of particular sensory experiences and guided observation upon writing?
11. At what stages of maturity do students spontaneously *seek* specific help in improving particular aspects of writing, such as specificity of details, transitions, parallel structure, and metaphor?
12. At which levels of maturation *can* particular aspects of writing most efficiently be learned?
13. Does the oral reading of rough drafts help the elementary school child strengthen "sentence sense"? How does it?
14. What techniques of composition most effectively help build self-discipline and pride in clarity, originality, and good form?
15. What procedures of teaching and learning composition are most effective for pupils of low socioeconomic patterns?
16. What procedures of teaching and learning composition are most effective for pupils learning to write English as a second language?
17. Can study of the newer types of linguistics help writers?
18. Can formal study of rhetorical theory or of logic help writers?
19. How is writing affected by extensive study and imitation or parody of models?
20. What forms of discourse have the greatest effect on other types of writing? For example, does writing poetry help a writer of reports?
21. What is involved in the act of writing?
22. How does a person go about starting a paper? What questions must he answer for himself?
23. How does a writer generate sentences?
24. Of what does skill in writing really consist?

SELECTED READINGS IN COMPOSITION

BAILEY, DUDLEY (ed.). *Essays on Rhetoric.* New York: Oxford University Press, 1965. For background, beginning teachers should read especially the following:
Aristotle — *The Rhetoric*
Cicero — *De Oratore, De Inventione*
Quintilianus — *Institutio Oratorio*
Hugh Blair — *Lectures on Rhetoric, Belles Lettres*
George Campbell — *The Philosophy of Rhetoric*
BELSKY, MANUEL. *Patterns of Argument.* New York: Holt, Rinehart and Winston, Inc., 1963.
BISSEX, HENRY. *Visuals for Composition.* Holyoke, Massachusetts: Technifax Corporation, 1965.
BRADDOCK, RICHARD, RICHARD LLOYD-JONES, and LOWELL SCHOER. *Research in Written Composition.* Champaign, Illinois: National Council of Teachers of English, 1963.
CHRISTENSEN, FRANCIS. *The Christensen Rhetoric Program.* Evanston, Illinois: Harper & Row, 1969.
CORBETT, EDWARD P. J. *Classical Rhetoric for the Modern Student.* New York: Oxford University Press, 1965.
JOOS, MARTIN. *The Five Clocks.* Bloomington, Indiana: Publication 22 of the Indiana University Research Center in Anthropology, Folklore, and Linguistics, 1962.
MILIC, LOUIS T. *Style and Stylistics, An Analytical Bibliography.* New York: The Free Press, 1967.
MOFFETT, JAMES. *Teaching the Universe of Discourse.* Boston: Houghton-Mifflin Co., 1968.
MURRAY, DONALD M. *A Writer Teaches Writing.* Boston: Houghton-Mifflin Co., 1968.
RICHARDS, I. A. *The Philosophy of Rhetoric.* New York: Oxford University Press, 1936.
RYLE, GILBERT. *Dilemmas.* Cambridge, England: Cambridge University Press, 1954.
SHERWOOD, JOHN C. *Discourse of Reason: A Brief Handbook of Semantics and Logic.* New York: Harper and Brothers, 1960.
SHUGRUE, MICHAEL F., and GEORGE HILLOCKS, JR. *Classroom Practices in Teaching English.* Champaign, Illinois: National Council of Teachers of English, 1965.
SMITH, EUGENE H. Director, "Rhetoric and School Programs." Papers from the NCTE Spring Institutes, reprinted from the *English Journal.* Champaign, Illinois: NCTE, April, 1966.
YOUNG, RICHARD T., ALTON L. BECKER, and KENNETH L. PIKE. *Rhetoric: Discovery and Change.* New York: Harcourt, Brace & World, Inc., 1970.

CHAPTER 6

A Miscellany Concerning the Teaching
of English and the Curriculum

THE ENGLISH TEACHER AND CENSORSHIP

Beginning teachers often have their enthusiasm dampened by reactionary communities which find fault with the literature which such teachers feel interest students and which the teachers have built into their plans. Such interference will often intimidate neophyte teachers, who may respond to it by leaving the profession or by giving up their plans and shifting to the use of more conventional and "safe" materials. However, what may be conventional materials for one community may be controversial ones in another. At one time *The Adventures of Huckleberry Finn* was attacked in many communities not as a racist book but as a vulgar and obscene one. Within the past decade there have been controversies over the teaching of *The Scarlet Letter.* Books such as *Catcher in the Rye, Lord of the Flies, To Kill a Mockingbird* — books which speak directly and strongly to youth and have much good in them — have been the center of controversy in many communities and the reason for discouragement or dismissal of many promising young teachers of English.

In reactionary communities where there have been complaints about the literature taught in the secondary school, administrators, sometimes fearful of their jobs, seldom take a stand with their boards of education to defend the teacher from the community. By fiat they often direct the teacher to discontinue teaching the book which is at the center of the dispute or the subject of a strong complaint. And if the teacher resists too strongly, he is usually not rehired if he is not summarily dismissed. Furthermore, if he resists, he may not get a fair recommendation from his administrator when he seeks another teaching position.

There seems to be scarcely any rhyme or reason why certain books are suspect in a particular community. One busybody in a community may create a difficult situation for a whole school system by protesting the school's teaching of certain titles. One person of this sort can often stir up a group of supporters to metamorphose a single complaint to a *cause célèbre*. Too often the person launching the complaint knows almost nothing about good literature and would condemn a very good modern novel or even an old *classic* simply because of a single word used in the text. The word *rape*, for example, caused the attack on *To Kill a Mockingbird* in one community. *Adultery* was the word which brought complaints against *The Scarlet Letter* in another.

THE ENGLISH TEACHER AND THE NATIONAL COUNCIL OF TEACHERS OF ENGLISH

The teacher of English should join his professional organization. Then if he should become the center of a controversy having to do with censorship, his organization can, even if in only an indirect way, come to his aid. In some states the state council of Teachers of English is a strong organization and often comes to the aid of individual teachers who are out of favor in reactionary communities. In 1962 the National Council of Teachers of English prepared a very useful pamphlet called *The Student's Right to Read*. This pamphlet alerts teachers to some of the capable writers and good books who and which have been attacked. It contains an open letter to citizens respecting one's right to read; it explains how censorship in most respects is a threat to education; and it attempts to explain the teacher's purposes in teaching what appears to some to be "immoral books." This pamphlet reminds the community of its responsibility to keep schools free from the interference and discord which an illiterate minority can impose upon it. One of the most useful parts of this pamphlet is a questionnaire which the teacher may ask the complainant to answer. The questions asked in this publication are so sensibly and strategically phrased that they tend to stop the complainant by making him see the error and weakness and shortsightedness of his position. And if they do not stop him, they at least formalize his charges and give the teacher and the school something more than a rumor to confront.

The beginning teacher should be a member of his professional organization, furthermore, because membership carries with it a subscription to the *English Journal*. Each issue is comprised of ten or more articles written by members of the profession and containing many useful suggestions in respect to materials, teaching strategies, and related matters. Reading this publication keeps the beginning teacher in touch with the direction in which the profession is moving, and it is a dynamic profession. In addition to the monthly journal, the NCTE has a great many booklets, monographs, and books available for teachers to purchase; and these can teach both the beginning and the experienced teachers a great deal. If the beginning teacher is experimentally minded and also one who would like to share his discoveries, his professional journal is there ready to publish his reports. Through such publication a beginning teacher may become known nationally. His opportunities for advancement are thus enhanced.

THE ENGLISH TEACHER AND THE
DARTMOUTH CONFERENCE

The Anglo-American Conference on the Teaching and Learning of English, held at Dartmouth College in 1966, has been extremely influential on American schools and teachers. The beginning teacher would do well to get acquainted with the issues which this conference evoked and to read the English view—John Dixon's *Growth Through English*[1]—and the American—Herbert J. Muller's *The Uses of English*[2]—of English and its teaching.

After four weeks of soul-searching discussion, the 50 participants reached a consensus on 11 points which continue to generate national, and international, debate:

1. The centrality of the pupil's exploring, extending, and shaping experiences in the English classroom.
2. The urgency of developing classroom approaches stressing the vital, creative, dramatic involvement of children and young people in language experiences.
3. The importance of directing more attention to speaking and listening experiences for all pupils at all levels, particularly those experiences which involve vigorous interaction among children.
4. The wisdom of providing young people at all levels with significant opportunities for the creative use of language: creative dramatics, imaginative writing, improvisation, role-playing, and similar activities.
5. The significance of rich literary experiences in the educative process and the importance of teachers of English restudying particular selections to determine their appropriateness for readers at different levels.

6. The need to overcome the restrictiveness of rigid patterns of "grouping" or "streaming" which limit the linguistic environment in which boys and girls learn English and which tend to inhibit language development.

7. The need to negate the limiting, often stultifying, impact of examination patterns which direct attention of both teachers and pupils to aspects of English which are at best superficial and often misleading.

8. The compelling urgency of improving the conditions under which English is taught in the schools: the need for more books and libraries, for better equipment, for reasonable class size, for a classroom environment which will make good teaching possible.

9. The importance of teachers of English at all levels informing themselves about the results of pertinent scholarship and research so that their classroom approaches may be guided accordingly.

10. The need for radical reform in programs of teacher education, both pre-service and in-service.

11. The importance of educating the public on what is meant by good English and what is meant by good English teaching.

The Dartmouth participants seemed intent on making English a more liberal, humane study, a task which might well require the re-education of most teachers, principals, superintendents, school boards — and parents — in America. They also subscribed to the idea that English should offer mature students works which present diverse visions of life, a wide range of choices from which students may be better prepared to select for themselves.

The seminar group as a whole reached agreement in being opposed to grouping students according to their ability. This type of classification usually ends in segregating the slow, the retarded, or those of another culture in classroom groups where they have no access to the more mature ideas of superior students. The group made a strong recommendation for a variety of students in the classroom.

The British and the Americans disputed what constitutes sequence in a subject or in education generally. The British believed that sequence is the order in the psychological development of the child, while the Americans tended to see sequence as an order built into the curriculum. Finally the two reached a compromise that "there is no one road, but many" in establishing what is meant by continuity.

Both British and American participants agreed that "English teachers need to have a sound, conscious knowledge of the language," but the British were wary of introducing the grammars into school curricula. Muller is strong for the schools to teach standard English to all students, since he believes that without a command of it poor children would be unable to compete equally in economic opportunities. Dixon, on the other hand, recommends that the teacher "make available a variety of situations in which, if the pupil chooses . . . knowledge may gradually become explicit and controllable."

One participant[3] summed up the discussions on literature in this way: "I think two trends-to-be were foreshadowed at Dartmouth. One was the teaching of literature as an engaging with life; the other was the teaching of literature through the instrumentalities of linguistics." American secondary-school teachers of English have been guilty of teaching biography and history instead of literature for a good many years. The use of anthologies of literature organized historically has encouraged this emphasis. The *New Criticism,* which appeared in the nineteen-thirties, has had some effect in getting teachers to treat literature as a fine art and of prime concern, and the historical place of the literary selection and the biography of its author as minor concerns.

We can undoubtedly attribute to the Dartmouth Conference the resurgence of interest in speaking and creative dramatics in the English classroom of American schools. For some time large high schools have tended to have an English department and a speech and drama department. But American teachers of English are becoming increasingly aware of how well speech and drama assist them in bringing their students into an active, creative involvement with language and in using literature as a representation of real life. They are, therefore, encouraging oral activities which get young people seriously engaged with language and literature and vigorously interacting with each other. This tendency and kind of activity also is quite likely responsible for the English teachers' relinquishing his domination of the classroom and using a strategy which not only puts students in the center of the learning activity but also tends to shift to them the responsibility for making education successful. Though the British schools and the American schools, as well as their teachers and students, may be quite dissimilar, it is obvious that the Dartmouth Conference has brought us newer insights. As for teaching literature "through the instrumentalities of linguistics," the Nebraska English Curriculum Study Center had already in 1962 anticipated the importance of this strategy: "It is a basic premise of this curriculum that probably the best basis for building a child's competence in composition and language is an exposure to literature of superior quality over a relatively long period of time." And the obverse, the best way to understand and appreciate literature is to see it as an exhibition of the use of language at its best.

The effect of the Dartmouth Conference was to stimulate a spate of experimentation in the secondary-school teaching of English as well as the elementary school's teaching of the language arts. Such experimentation is usually good, since some of the most significant discoveries about a discipline and its teaching come out of such experimentation.

THE TEACHER OF ENGLISH AND MEDIA RESOURCES

At one time books and an occasional periodical were the only teaching materials available to the teacher of English, but with the "electronic revolution" have come a great many tools and materials which enhance the teaching of English: literature, language, and composition.

The film has become increasingly important in the teaching of literature. Before 1960 there were very few films of real merit available to the English teacher. Then the Massachusetts Council for the Humanities under the direction of Floyd Rinker set a standard for films for the teaching of literature which few have been able to equal since. This undertaking has had a good effect on the commercial makers of films; it has spurred them to achieve top quality in their preparation of films for educational purposes. The Massachusetts Council for the Humanities originally produced 12 30-minute films, three groups with sets of four: The Classical Greek Tragedy set—Oedipus Rex, Age of Sophocles; Oedipus Rex, The Character of Oedipus; Oedipus Rex, Man and God; and Oedipus Rex, The Recovery of Oedipus. The Elizabethan drama set was comprised of the following: Hamlet, the Age of Elizabeth; Hamlet, The Poisoned Kingdom; Hamlet, The Readiness Is All; and Hamlet, What Happens in Hamlet. The Humanities series was comprised of the Humanities, What They Are and What They Do; The Theatre, One of the Humanities; Thornton Wilder, Our Town and Ourselves. These films were prepared for televising in the late nineteen-fifties. In the early nineteen-sixties they were sold to Encyclopaedia Britannica, which has distributed them since. To this group of 12 films Encyclopaedia Britannica[4] has added about 17 more films, all high in literary merit and almost equal in quality to the first 12. Teachers find all of these films very useful in reinforcing the teaching of literature.

Schools also have available to them a great many films produced for the general public but satisfactory for school use. Representatives among these are such films as *Abe Lincoln in Illinois, Arsenic and Old Lace, The Barretts of Wimpole Street, The Bridges at Toko-Ri, The Brothers Karamazov, Captains Courageous, Charge of the Light Brigade, A Christmas Carol, David Copperfield, Citizen Kane,* and many more.[5]

Films for the teaching of language also are available and valuable aids to a teacher who is likely to feel the need of an expert to reinforce his teaching. One of the first series is that made and narrated by Henry Lee Smith, University of New York at Buffalo, a natural performer. "Language and Linguistics" is comprised of twelve 30-minute presentations produced in the early nineteen-sixties and presently distributed by Indiana University. The Oregon Curriculum Study Center also prepared an excellent series on transformational grammar with Wayne O'Neil as teacher. These are distributed by McGraw-Hill, Inc., New York.

Perhaps of even greater excellence than the commercial films are many of the recordings which various companies have made for educational use. These recordings engage our best actors and actresses to record poetry, drama, short stories, and even some novels. Almost any selection that a teacher might want to use is available. The beginning teacher should ask recording companies for copies of their catalogs.

Recordings are not limited to the teaching of literature. There are a number which focus on the teaching of language. The Yale University Press has available Helge Kökeritz's "Shakespeare's Pronunciation." Available through the NCTE (Catalog No. 93801 R) is Harry Morgan Ayers' reading of selections from *Beowulf,* Chaucer, *et al.* with explanations of the changing sounds of the English language. The NCTE (No. 27401 R) also has available the Niel K. Snortum and Daniel Knapp's presentation of English as spoken in Chaucer's day in contrast with that spoken today. Another useful record is John Dunn's "The Changing English Language (93909 R). John Muri and Raven McDavid have made a record called "Americans Speaking" (24306 R). This discourse representing six American dialects is also distributed by the NCTE. The foregoing are not all of the recordings of language available to the teacher, but these are among the best ones. They are particularly useful for the teacher who has had little training in the history or phonology of language or in American dialects, since these recordings, and also tapes, can bring to the ears of students discriminations in language change and among contemporary dialects which the teacher might be unable to represent accurately. Good recordings have a reliability which is not always available to students. Each language/rhetoric book in the Oregon series also included a short recording: Grade 7—"Varieties of English" (samples of regional dialects) and "Features of Sounds" (phonological patterns), etc. These are distributed by Holt, Rinehart & Winston.

The kinescope is another medium which has been used to improve the teaching of English. The Commission on English of the College Entrance Examination Board[6] prepared a series of 11 kinescopes during the nineteen-sixties. Four of these were[7] directed to the teaching of composition; one to grammar[8]; and six to literature.[9] All are of good quality; a few are extremely useful yet, particularly the four on aspects of composition.

The past decade has also seen the growth of television as a teaching medium. Both commercial and educational television have been productive, the commercial not so much as the educational, since its timing is seldom right for the classroom. Many school systems have used closed-circuit television, and more are using it than ever before. Closed-circuit television makes it possible for a single teacher who is very skillful and knowledgeable to affect a relatively large audience of students. However, schools find that this form of instruction should not be exclusive. Students also need the face-to-face confrontation of, and the interchange of ideas with, the classroom teacher that is absent from the television presentation. Large group lectures followed by small group discussions work well and complement each other.

Certain universities and educational institutions have been responsible for the development of a considerable library of video tapes which can be borrowed or rented. The University of Nebraska,[10] a pioneering institution in television instruction, has prepared a good many video tapes which are widely used. For a relevant list, see the bibliography at the end of this chapter.

The commercial television programs have also been useful. In the past decade a number of excellent presentations of Shakespearean plays and dramatizations of good novels have reinforced the teaching of English. Beginning teachers cannot afford to overlook the opportunities which commercial television gives them to reinforce their teaching of literature and language. When television programs are of good quality, students tend to watch them. The teacher needs to watch too so that he can discuss with his students these programs which are relevant to his discipline.

Marshall McLuhan has prophesied that our age is rapidly shifting its dependence on books to other media, particularly the audio-visual. As we watch television acquire an even greater audience, we are almost persuaded that McLuhan may be a genuine prophet. Whether he is right or wrong, the teacher should capitalize on those media and their programs which tend to make the teaching of literature and language a more effective experience. He should be aware of the possibilities for improved education inherent in audio-visual media.

The computer is being used by many schools to do the class scheduling and the record-keeping of a school system. In some schools the computer is helping to teach children how to read and high-school students how to increase their reading speed and understanding. In mathematics and science the computer is useful. There is a possibility that it may become equally useful in teaching students the nature of English grammar, particularly the generative possibilities inherent in syntax.

Tape recorders are also being used widely in schools. In some instances entire class discussions are recorded so that absent students may make up their losses more easily. Tape recorders are freeing young people from the pencil in the composition process. By dictating their oral composition to a tape recorder and then playing it back, young people have an opportunity to examine more carefully their compositions, make the necessary revisions, and then, as they put them in written form, to reduce the amount of time that the process demands when it is done completely through writing. Tape recorders are being used to teach pronunciation, vocabulary, to improve spelling. Teachers are finding it easier to tell a student where his weaknesses and strengths are in his composition by dictating to a tape recorder or a voice-writer than they are in finding the time for preparing adequate written comments. The real evaluation of a composition does not lie in the marginal code letters which teachers have conventionally written on students' papers to call attention to the minor writing offenses. It lies in the careful evaluation of the writers' stance, the implications of his audience, the substance of his communication, and the appropriateness of his style. To write of these matters on a student's composition takes far more time than any teacher of English has, particularly when he is attempting to teach four or five sections of English with 100 to 180 students in them.

The overhead projector and the opaque projector are also aids which enhance the teaching of English. Transparencies which demonstrate essay organization, teach students how to proofread and revise, help them focus on the prosodic characteristics of a specific poem; look at the floor plans of an Elizabethan stage, or view a sketch of the interior of the Globe theater can help the young teacher to make a professional presentation in his classroom. A case in point is the new rhetoric program developed by Professor Francis Christensen and transferred to an elaborate series of transparencies for the overhead projector. (This is distributed by Harper-Row, Evanston, Ill.) In this program the verbal is made visible.

For many students viewing a picture is a more successful way of learning than is reading a book. Such students find still pictures, as well as those in motion, meaningful in the educational process. Both still pictures, which can be projected on a screen by means of the opaque projector, and strip films, which are also projected, are useful teaching devices when a competent teacher puts them to use.

With the multi-media available to him and serving effectively to teach in a variety of ways, the young teacher should not underestimate his importance in the classroom. The media unstudied and used haphazardly can have little value for students. But when the teacher determines how to use them intelligently to enhance his teaching or to do things which the oral or written language cannot do, then he is proving how irreplaceable he really is. The teacher has to work relentlessly to discover how young people learn and how he can make that use of audio-visual aids which will promote the learning processes.

THE ENGLISH TEACHER AND THE INDIVIDUALIZED CURRICULUM

The more productive of the English curriculum study centers have made their programs available to school systems and teachers. Most of these programs are formally structured; three have been crystalized in graded textbooks and are being distributed by commercial publishers: the Oregon materials by Holt, Rinehart and Winston; the Carnegie-Mellon materials by Noble and Noble; and the Hunter College materials by Macmillan. Just as these materials began to be used by school systems, along came the Dartmouth Conference. The substance of this conference and particularly the British view toward structured curricula have undoubtedly been responsible for the fact that probably 10 percent of the secondary schools in the nation have been willing to adopt any structured curriculum in which they did not have an important, creative role. If one can detect a trend which began in the mid-nineteen-sixties and still continues, it is a trend to tailor English programs for a particular school clientele.

Most of us are familiar with the struggle which black students have made to get schools to set up specific courses in black literature or to incorporate in contemporary literature courses representative selections of black writers. The movement certainly is in the right direction if black students are to have a sense that English programs in the schools have relevance to them. To a lesser extent the Chicano and the American Indian minorities are working for similar treatment, and schools with heavy enrollments of students from minority groups are seriously attempting to meet the demands. Insofar as they succeed, they are likely to improve their holding power and reduce the number of drop-outs. An English program which seems unaware of any culture but that of the WASP has little attraction for students from minority cultures.

Besides trying to provide meaningful curricula for racial minorities, many schools are trying to prepare curricula which fit schools with a greater homogeneity of students. Such schools should be congratulated for refusing to cater to a mythical average student and for seriously studying the composition of their student body in order to meet the individual interests and needs more successfully.

One way in which some schools have attempted to meet the diverse interests and needs of their students has been to provide a large variety of elective courses from which students can select what collectively might constitute their secondary-school English program. Donald F. Weise at Wayne State University conceived such a program which he calls APEX (A Phase Elective English Program). The program offers students a wide range of elective courses in English, from easy to challenging, lasting from two weeks to a semester. Trenton, Michigan, High School has tried out this program and, in spite of some scheduling difficulty, has seen merit in it, since it has generated a more serious climate in English classes than ever existed before, and the holding power of the school has increased.

David B. Bronson of Lincoln-Sudbury Regional High School, Sudbury, Massachusetts, also has developed an elective English program for that school. To make the learning experience a more individualized one, he reduced the teachers' load from five classes a day and five days a week to four classes a day for four days a week. This plan releases teachers so that they may have one full day a week to set up individual conferences with their students. This individualizes instruction far more than it is possible to do in the conventional five classes a day for five days of the week. Here follow the course listings which students at Lincoln-Sudbury are offered.

BASIC READING AND WRITING (665)

Study Techniques
Vocabulary
Words and Their Ways
Notetaking
English Fundamentals

Reading for College
Reading Improvement
Transformational Grammar
Public Speaking
Debating

SPECIAL WRITING (492)

Creative
Short Story
Poetry

Expository
Yearbook

FILM (204)

What's in a Film
Visual Communication

No, but I Saw the Movie
Filmmaking

DRAMA (392)

TV Production
Acting
Stagecraft

Drama Workshop
Shakespeare

SPECIAL INTERESTS (1110)

Mythology
Growing Up in the '60s
Visions of Utopia
In Search of an Idea
Symposium
Demons in Literature
Introduction to Philosophy

Science Fiction
The World of Fantasy
Psychology and Literature
Voices in Controversy
Encounters—Not Making It
The Shape of Things to Come

LITERATURE (631)

Black Literature
British Satire
American Satire
John Steinbeck

Modern Poetry
American Literature
Short Stories of America
Bible as Literature

The Jazz Age
British Literature
Great Books

Omaha North High School[11] has been trying out an elective curriculum in English with reasonable success. Lincoln Southeast High School[12] set aside a two-week period between semesters in which students could elect from a body of short courses which the English faculty felt prepared to offer, and found that students responded to this program enthusiastically. Dunbar High School, Washington,

D.C.,[13] developed a literature program which gave students the opportunity to determine what literature they would study. At Hickory Township High School,[14] Sharon, Pennsylvania, the English department discarded a traditional program of six long courses, a semester for each, and substituted 32 short courses and gave students permission to sign up for whichever ones they wanted to study. The elective program does not, however, have to be structured in a large high school. Even small communities[15] report success with it.

Of course, in such elective courses there is a danger that some students will not get a clear conception of what literature is; but then there are students in traditional English courses who never respond to the literature being studied. Perhaps the risks are no greater in an elective program — where the school stands the chance of getting more interested participation by its students — than in a set and highly structured curriculum where only part of the class clientele feels a real sense of participation.

These elective courses are not restricted solely to the study of literature. They may be as elementary as short courses in spelling improvement or longer and more challenging courses in the composition of poetry. They may be in letter-writing or argumentative writing. They may be concerned with the study of local dialect or with transformational grammar. Elective courses of the kind to which we have been referring attempt to meet the needs, interests, and abilities of a wide range of students.

The elective curriculum in English may simply be a phase in the schools' moving from traditional programs to those with more awareness of contemporary culture. The beginning teacher needs to know that such a shift is taking place in some areas of the United States. This section of the final chapter has been included here not as an endorsement of elective-course programs but simply to inform the beginning teacher who may find himself employed by a school system experimenting with such a structure of English.

THE ENGLISH TEACHER AND HIS PREPARATION

Although there were a good many reasons why more and better prepared teachers of English were in demand in the nineteen-sixties, two reasons were paramount. The tremendous increase in young people of high-school age was one. The other was the increased attention to the "new grammars." Recently it was estimated that 125,000 secondary-school teachers teach English. Since as a whole schools require the study of English by all of their students for most of the years they are in school, educators came to realize that English is the greatest single force in the schools for liberating the imagination of students through literary experiences and for helping to develop their language abilities. After Sputnik the federal government, thinking pragmatically, became involved in retraining teachers of mathematics and the physical sciences. The National Defense Education Act provided a large sum of money to set up both summer and year-long programs for the training and/or retraining of such teachers. Recognizing that their role in national defense was equally worthy, English teachers agitated for equal privileges. In early 1965, the federal legislature enlarged the NDEA to include English, as well as other subjects, in the training programs supported by the federal government. Thus, between 1965 and 1969 there were 30 to 50 summer institutes annually for the retraining of English language arts teachers, a greater number for the secondary-school teachers than for the elementary-school ones.

The Commission on English of the College Entrance Examination Board had conducted a number of English institutes in the summer of 1962 for the retraining of English teachers, and the pattern for these institutes had considerable influence on the pattern of the NDEA Institutes in English. The Commission on English Institutes concentrated on three areas: literature, language, and composition. And since the new grammar was almost unknown to secondary-school English teachers, with the exception of a few pioneering ones,[16] the NDEA Institutes in English were crucial, therefore, in training a great many teachers in structural and transformational grammar and in encouraging them to disseminate this information in their schools. If one estimates that there were approximately 30 institutes each summer from 1965 through 1969, a period of five years, and the average membership of secondary-school English teachers was 25, we can multiply $30 \times 25 \times 5$ (years) and discover that about 3,750 teachers were trained in some kind of new grammar. With 125,000 secondary-school English teachers as the estimated total, a group of 3,750 constitute a very small percentage of the total number, most of whom needed training. The federal program was helpful but in the long run scarcely a drop in the bucket to what the needs were then and what they still are.

If the beginning teacher discovers that the school where he has been elected to teach has no one who is teaching one of the new grammars, he will have to proceed tactfully if he has been trained in the field and try to get the school to allow him to do in-service training of other English teachers so that ultimately the school can change over. It is not likely that the beginning teacher should undertake this strategy during his first year. He needs first to establish himself with his colleagues and have their trust. In the interim the beginning teacher might well omit all instruction in grammar, except what he can bootleg into the classroom, rather than to inflict the traditional grammar on students. Such time might be better spent in studying literature, in composing, or in dealing with other aspects of language — the history of the English language, dialectology, semantics, lexicography.

Even though most teacher-training schools know that traditional English language programs are outmoded, some such schools have not brought their curricula up to date. If the beginning teacher is a graduate from such an institution, he will need to begin to make up for that deprivation. Chapter 4 of this book contains recommendations as to how he can go about doing this. In addition he can seek the help of an experienced colleague who has been a participant in an NDEA Institute in English or who has, by personal study and summer-school attendance, managed to inform himself.

Some schools arrange for in-service training of their English teachers. A beginning teacher should be aware of such a possibility and, if given an opportunity, might suggest to the superintendent or his immediate superior the possibility of bringing in a specialist in linguistics from a local college or nearby state university to offer such a course to him and his colleagues. To train teachers in linguistics is especially crucial, since understanding new approaches to composition, to dialectology and usage, and even to prosody is dependent on a knowledge of linguistics.

Finally, we might mention again to the beginning teacher that a subscription to his major professional publication is one means by which he can become better educated in respect to all aspects of English — its content and its teaching. And attendance at state or national conventions of English teachers can be both practical and inspirational. The field of English is so wide and diverse that it is large and interesting enough to attract a lifetime of dedication.

SELECTED BIBLIOGRAPHY OF AUDIO-VISUAL AIDS

Recordings

In addition to the recording which the teacher will find listed in the NCTE publication, *Resources,* he might also write to the following companies for their listing of records:

Argo Record Company, Ltd., 113 Fulham Road, London, SW 3.
Audio-Classic, 200 Park Avenue, New York, New York, 10003 (many novels
     as well as plays).
Columbia Masterworks, 51 W. 52nd St., New York, New York, 10019.
Decca Records, Inc., 50 West 57 Street, New York, New York.
Educational Materials Division, 180 East 6th Street, St. Paul, Minnesota,
     55101.
Folkway Record, 121 West 47 Street, New York, New York.
The Library of Congress Recording Laboratory, Library of Congress, Wash-
     ington, D.C.
The McGraw Hill Record Library, Spoken Arts, Inc., New Rochelle, New
     York, 10801.

Resources for the Teaching of English, 1971-72 (published annually), Urbana,
     Illinois, 1111 Kenyon Road, NCTE — listings of recordings, film strips,
     media study, literary maps)
Shakespeare Recording Society Inc., 505 8th Avenue, New York, New York,
     10018.
Yale University Press, New Haven, Connecticut, 06520.

Films

For teachers interested in the film as educational medium, they might
subscribe to the following periodical:

Audio Visual Instruction, A publication by the Department of Audio Visual
     Instruction, National Education Association. Published monthly.

Here follows a listing of valuable books for the teacher to read in preparing himself to use the film for educational purposes:

BLUESTONE, GEORGE. *Novels into Films.* 1961. (Berkeley: University of Cali-
     fornia Press, $1.95). 237 pp. A good study for the English teacher.
     Analyzes the techniques appropriate to literature and to films. Book-film
     combinations under study are: *The Informer, Pride and Prejudice, The
     Ox-Bow Incident, Grapes of Wrath, Madame Bovary,* and *Wuthering
     Heights.*
CULKIN, JOHN, S.J. *Julius Caesar: As a Play and as a Film.* 1963 (New York:
     Scholastic Books). 186 pp. Paper. The text of Shakespeare's play with a
     case study of the way in which the stage and the screen media treat the
     material.
_____. *The Motion Picture as an Art Form, Film Study in the High School
     (Catholic High School Quarterly,* Vd. XXIII, No. 3, October, 1955).
KNIGHT, ARTHUR. *The Liveliest Art.* 1957 (New York: Mentor Books, MD 263,
     50¢). 352 pp. A good popular study of the history of film around the world
     up to 1957. Contains an annoted bibliography of 100 books of film.

MCANANY, EMILE, S.J., and ROBERT WILLIAMS, S.J. *The Filmviewer's Handbook,* 1965. (New York: Paulist Press, Deus Books, 95¢). 208 pp. Fine, practical introduction to the what and how of establishing a film-study group. Includes a short history of film, an analysis of film techniques, a sample film series, and source information on books and films.

MALLERY, DAVID. *The School and the Art of Motion Pictures.* 1966. (Boston: National Association of Independent Schools, 7904 Germantown Ave., Philadelphia, Pennsylvania, 19118). 102 pp. A lively, articulate and practical study on the many roles of film in the schools. Contains brief comments on a large number of films and on the places within the curriculum where films can be used and studied.

National Council of Teachers of English. *Motion Pictures and the Teachings of English.* 1965. (New York: Appleton-Century-Crofts) A very readable and useful book to introduce the English teacher to the place of motion pictures within the curriculum. Excellent analyses of *Grapes of Wrath, Citizen Kane,* and *The Miracle Worker.*

Videotapes

ENGLISH LITERATURE

Books Before Gutenberg
Dante and Others
Dr. Johnson and Keats
English in a Decade of Change
Historical Novel
The Immigrant Novel in America
Jonathan Swift
Modern Poetry
Neihardt on Creative Writing
Poeming
The R of It (Developmental Reading)
Religion of Shakespeare
The Role of the Poet: Politics and the Artist
The Short Story
The Short Story—Katherine Anne Porter
Understanding the Fine Arts
War Novels: Yesterday, Today, and Tomorrow

The following list is available from the Nebraska Educational Television Council for Higher Education, Inc., 1800 North 33rd Street, Lincoln, Nebraska.

ENGLISH CURRICULUM

English in a Decade of Change

ENGLISH LANGUAGE

Exploring Edges of Language
Language: Form and Meaning I
Language: Form and Meaning II
Language Stages and Styles
Linguistics in Teaching of the Disadvantaged
Poverty, Language, and Learning
The R of It (Developmental Reading)
Two English Languages
Various American Dialects

Audio Visual Miscellany

The following is a recommended selection of films which Patrick Hazard, Chairman, English Department, Beaver College, made on his completion of an investigation during 1966-67 of the best educational films then available for use in NDEA English institutes. This investigation was financed by a federal grant.

I. Specially recommended: "Benito Cereno" by Robert Lowell, NET A-V, 1 hour and 40 minutes, write Mr. James Cole, NET A-V, Bloomington, Indiana, call (812) 337-2002.

   Columbia Records sells an LP of the American Place Theatre production of "Benito Cereno." There are two excellent casebooks available for the study of *Benito Cereno*, Seymour Gross's for Wadsworth Publishing Company (Belmont, California) and Joseph P. Runden's for D. C.Heath (Boston, Massachusetts). These gathered materials plus the 30-odd sources cited on the tale and its provenance in Jarvis Thurston, *et al., Short Story Criticism*, pp. 155-56, provide the media-shy instructor with a way of digging deeply, at one and the same time, into a neglected classic of great timeliness and a major contemporary poet's creative dialog with his intellectual ancestor. Sourcebook, novel, LP, TV play, contemporary critical reaction provide the easily accessible materials for an in-depth study of the interactions between media and literature.

II. The following represent the best newer media materials touching a wide range of genres and literary themes.

While we prefer studying intensively one work like the Lowell-Melville transaction in *Benito Cereno,* we believe night-time screenings of a less rigorous nature would provide institute participants with epiphanies of their own about how to use newer media as literary vehicles in their own right. Because films on painting perhaps need a separate rationale, we provide a brief defense of their inclusion.

Literature more frequently than not is taught in a cultural vacuum in the high schools. There is Bryant without Cole; Emerson but no Greenough; Howells but no Hopper. Salinger is read, but Levine, equally disturbed by the repressively phony, is rarely seen.

This defect in our search for cultivation in the schools is in part due to teacher ignorance, in part to the relative inaccessibility of non-print arts. Good films like *Yankee Painter* and *Jack Levine* (both Contemporary Films), interesting nonfiction works in their own right, are ideal esthetic structures for eliciting mature acts of written criticism. More than that, however, such films relieve teacher and student alike — at one and the same time — of corrigible ignorance about the total cultural milieu which alone makes possible the fullest comprehension of a literary work.

POETRY

"In a Dark Time," 40 minutes, Contemporary Films, 267 West 25th Street, New York, 10001, $15.00 rental. Theodore Roethke reads his verse.

"A Child's Christmas in Wales," 26 minutes, Contemporary, $10.00 rental. Sensitive animation of still photography.

Albert Waller at WCBS-TV (245 W. 55th Street, New York, New York, 10019) has matched last year's achievement ("In the American Grain: William Carlos Williams") with a splendid mosaic on New York as seen by its writers from Whitman to Updike, "Sense of the City." For free loan of both half hour films, write George Dessart at WCBS-TV, 9th floor.

The NCTE sponsored a Festival of Films on Poetry in Houston. Television Information Office prepared a free brochure commenting on the films. TIO, 745 Fifth Avenue, New York City.

FICTION

"Faulkner's Mississippi," 50 minutes, Benchmark Films, 516 Fifth Avenue, New York, 10035, (212) MU2-4777. Brilliant evocation of the small town and hunting mileux of Yoknapatawpha.

"Dickens' England," 25 minutes, Encyclopaedia Britannica Films, Wilmette, Illinois. Excellent period graphics evoke the Victorian ambience of Dickens' fiction.

"Sense of the City," 28 minutes, WCBS-TV, limited free loan. A literary mosaic of great power about New York City.

DRAMA

"Who Do You Kill?", 50 minutes, Carousel Films, 1501 Broadway, New York, 10019, (212) LA4-4126. East Side/West Side TV film on rat-bite infanticide in Harlem.

"No Hiding Place," 50 minutes, Carousel Films. Integration in a polite Long Island suburb.

"In White America," Columbia LP of off-Broadway play about the history of slavery, by Princeton historian Martin Duberman. Signet paperback.

NONFICTION

"My Childhood," 50 minutes, Benchmark Films. Parallel autobiographies of James Baldwin and Hubert Humphrey.

"Images of Leonard Baskin," 28 minutes, Contemporary Films. Rental $22.50. Eloquent self-appraisal of the esthetic of a leading American printmaker.

"Marked for Failure," 55 minutes, NET audio-visual service, Bloomington, Indiana. Rental $9.15. Excellent study of compensatory education strategies in center-city schools.

Two of America's most talented young film directors, Michael Roemer and Robert Young, have produced *Nothing but a Man,* the first film to handle the racial crisis as a human rather than a sociological problem. It is now available on 16mm rental. These ex-English majors will inspire our students to use the newer media eloquently and responsibly. Write George Dessart at WCBS-TV, 9th floor.

The Dartmouth Conference on Film Study in the college premiered a sampler of prize-winning student film circulated by the National Student Associations, Washington. For rates and other valuable suggestions, apply to David Stewart, National Foundation on the Arts, 1800 G Street, NW, Washington, D.C.

Viewers at the Anglo-American Seminar on the Teaching and Learning of English at Dartmouth were particularly impressed by three films distributed by Contemporary Films (267 W. 25th Street, New York City, 10001):

"Clay," a short experimental animated film on the short and not exceedingly happy life of *homo sapiens* – 10 minutes.

"Very Nice, Very Nice," an expressionist parable about complacency in the atomic age—6 minutes.

"John Hirsch," a half-hour analysis of one man's successful campaign to bring community theater to Winnipeg, Canada.

III. Contact Mr. Ed Lamb, TV Office, room 1626, Standard Oil of New Jersey, Rockefeller Center, New York, (212) 974-3000, for free use in your NDEA Summer Institutes along the Eastern seaboard from Maine to Puerto Rico.

1. Esso Repertory Theatre—single prints available.

2. World Theatre—three prints available.

3. Festival of Performing Arts—three prints available.

Esso Repertory Theatre

1. "Irish Triple Bill: *(Calvary,* Yeats; *How He Lied to Her Husband,* Shaw; *Act Without Words II,* Beckett), Playhouse in the Park, Cincinnati.

2. "Bedtime Story," Sean O'Casey, Seattle Repertory Theatre.

3. "The Dumb Waiter," Harold Pinter, Hull House Theatre, Chicago.

4. "St. Patrick's Day," Richard Brinsley Sheridan, The Charles Playhouse, Boston.

5. "The Creditors," August Strindberg, Barter Theatre, Abingdon, Virginia.

6. "Don Juan in Hell," George Bernard Shaw, APA at the Phoenix, New York City.

7. "A Wedding," Anton Chekov, Milwaukee Repertory Theatre.

8. "Chee-Chee" and "The Man with the Flower in His Mouth," Luigi Pirandello, The Theatre Group, University of California Extension, Los Angeles.

9. "Trojan Women," Euripides, Alley Theatre, Houston, Texas.

The appearance in *TV as Art: Some Essays in Criticism* (NCTE, $1.25) of Richard Stonesifer's comparative explication of the American and Nigeria items in Esso World Theatre make these two films particularly germane to connected TV study with literary criticism.

National Educational Television did English a great service this past year by running its *U.S.A. Literature* series. For a complete catalog, write Dr. James A. Cole, NET Films Audio Visual Center, Indiana University, Bloomington.

Afterword

Schools are caught in the middle of a far-reaching cultural change. A teacher beginning his professional career at this time may be mystified, perhaps confused, by finding himself involved in adjusting to various kinds of changes for which his academic preparation has not equipped him. The following comes from an unsolicited letter from a former student, a lady who has taught secondary-school English for the past ten years. She teaches in one of the 12 largest cities in the United States, in an all-white suburb of that city. A paragraph of her letter is reproduced here in order to give the reader some impressions of the kinds of problems which may confront him as he enters the teaching profession.

Many of you who are involved in the world of teaching will understand when I say that all is not well in the field of education. At a time when change is needed in the educational process we find the teachers and students moving in one direction while the public at large is moving in an opposite direction. We have almost been sickened by the word "accountability" for it seems to mean that standaridized testing is on its way, and no one I know has ever seen a standardized test which was a valid test of much of anything. In addition, we are told that we are accountable for our students' learning, but we are to have no voice in the conditions under which they learn: class size, course offerings, textbooks selections, number of students per day, number of course preparations per teacher, and materials which may be used. I don't want to be accountable for conditions over which I have no control. I'll accept my accountability when the teachers, the students, the school board, and the administrators, plus the community accept their fair share in the whole process. I have long had a mind set against a stacked deck. We are faced again this year with possible teacher lay-offs during the school year since the state legislature has been unable to come up with a definite state-aid formula — we lost 70 teachers from the system last year. The integration problem with bussing and all of the

93

other emotional things which surround this issue have also hit our school system. Perhaps some of you have read of Judge_____'s decision regarding the_____schools. The current wage-price fiasco has contributed to the low morale too—we are presently battling this one in the courts since we did have a contract before August 14. Being on the executive board of our_____Education Association has brought me right into the middle of all of this, and perhaps most frustrating of all is trying to educate the people we are fighting for.

Notes

CHAPTER 3

1. "Teacher's Manual," *Gateway English* (New York: The Macmillan Company), pp. 1 ff.

2. You might also consult the following: *A Guide to Available Project English Materials*, NCTE-ERIC, edited by Donna Bulter and Bernard O'Donnell (Champaign, Illinois (now Urbana): NCTE, October, 1968).

CHAPTER 4

1. See bibliography at chapter end.

2. K. T. Fann, *Ludwig Wittgenstein: The Man and His Philosophy*, Delta paperback (5116-5), (Dell Publishing Company).

3. J. L. Austin and Gilbert Ryle.

4. See *Language Exploration for the Elementary Grades* (Lincoln, Nebraska: University of Nebraska Press, 1967).

5. This unit classifies as both *grammar* and *meaning;* it demonstrates how rhetoric evolves from grammar.

6. These units classify as both *grammar* and *meaning;* they demonstrate how rhetoric evolves from grammar.

CHAPTER 5

1. Richard Braddock *et al., Research in Written Composition* (Champaign, Illinois: National Council of Teachers of English, 1963).

2. Virginia M. Burke, "Opening Remarks," *Emerging Outlines of a New Rhetoric* (Oshkosh, Wisconsin: Wisconsin Council of Teachers of English, 1966).

3. See "Introduction," *A Curriculum for English,* Grade One (Lincoln, Nebraska: University of Nebraska Press, 1967).

4. See also the Nebraska English Curriculum, "The Rhetoric of Literature," Units 71 and 72.

5. See also the Nebraska English Curriculum, "The Rhetoric of Literature," Unit 89.

6. *English Sentences* (New York: Harcourt, Brace and World, 1962), Chapter 19.

7. *Toward a New Rhetoric* (Chicago: Harper-Row, 1967).

8. S. I. Hayakawa, *Language in Thought and Action,* 2nd ed. (New York: Harcourt, Brace and World, 1941).

9. Vol. 60, No. 8 (November, 1971).

CHAPTER 6

1. Reading, England: National Association for the Teaching of English, 1967.

2. New York: Holt, Rinehart & Winston, Inc., 1967.

3. Arthur Eastman, "Trends in Teaching Literature," *The Future of the English Curriculum,* ed. by James Barry (New York: 1967), p. 4.

4. See a film catalog of Encyclopaedia Britannica for a listing (1150 Wilmette Avenue, Wilmette, Illinois, 60091).

5. See the catalog of FILMS, Inc. (4420 Oakton Street, Skokie, Illinois).

6. 687 Boylston Street, Boston, Massachusetts, 02116.

7. "A Student Writing Assignment Based on 'Fire Walking in Ceylon,'" by Arthur Carr; "*The Speaking Voice* and the Teaching of Composition," by Walker Gibson; "Invention and Topics, or Where to Look for Something to Say," by Scott Elledge; "Organization — Rhetorical and Artistic," by George Williams.

8. "Grammar and Generative Grammar," by Karl V. Teter.

9. "Teaching a Poem," by Leonard Wolf; "A Class Study of Roethke's 'The Waking,'" by Alice C. Coleman; "Teaching Biography in the Secondary School," by Darcy Curwen; "Teaching Shakespeare's 'Henry IV, Part One,'" by Hallet Smith; "Teaching a Short Story: Faulkner's 'Barn Burning,'" by Sarah Youngblood; and "Teaching a Novel: *Moby Dick* in the Classroom," by Terence Martin.

10. See *Instructional Materials Catalog,* Vol. 3, 1971-72, NETCHE (Nebraska Education Council for Higher Education).

11. Frank Hobbs, Chairman of the English Department, speaking informally.

12. Mary C. Commers, "Operation English Freedom," *English Journal* (Champaign, Illinois: NCTE, May, 1970).

13. Lorraine Goldman, "Reading and Reporting: A Tailor-Made Program for Each Student," *English Journal,* Vol. 58, No. 2 (February, 1969).

14. Jack E. Smith, Jr., "180 Days: Observation of an Elective Year," *English Journal,* Vol. 60, No. 2 (February, 1971).

15. Thomas H. Morton and Mario P. Dei Dolori, *English Journal,* Vol. 60, No. 7 (October, 1971).

16. Miriam Goldstein, Newton, Massachusetts, High School, and Louise Higgins, Westport, Connecticut, Public Schools were two of the most outstanding ones.

General Bibliography

BRADDOCK, RICHARD, *et al. Research in Written Composition.* Champaign, Illinois: National Council of Teachers of English, 1963.

BURKE, VIRGINIA M. "Opening Remarks," *Emerging Outlines of a New Rhetoric.* Oshkosh, Wisconsin: Wisconsin Council of Teachers of English, 1966.

BUTLER, DONNA (ed.). *A Guide to Available Project English Materials.* Champaign, Illinois: NCTE-ERIC, October, 1968.

CHRISTENSEN, FRANCIS. *Toward a New Rhetoric.* Chicago: Harper-Row, 1967.

COMMERS, MARY C. "Operation English Freedom," *English Journal.* Champaign, Illinois: NCTE, May, 1970.

DIXON, JOHN. *Growth Through English.* Reading, England: National Association for the Teaching of English, 1967.

EASTMEN, ARTHUR. "Trends in Teaching Literature," *The Future of the English Curriculum.* Ed. by James Barry. New York: 1967. P. 4.

English Journal. Champaign, Illinois: National Council of Teachers of English (November, 1971), Vol. 60, No. 8.

FANN, K. T. *Ludwig Wittgenstein: The Man and His Philosophy.* Delta (5116-5). Dell Publishing Company.

GOLDMAN, LORRAINE. "Reading and Reporting: A Tailor-Made Program for Each Student," *English Journal.* Champaign, Illinois (February, 1969), Vol. 58, No. 2.

HAYAKAWA, S. I. *Language in Thought and Action,* second edition. New York: Harcourt, Brace and World, 1941.

Instructional Materials Catalog. Lincoln, Nebraska: Nebraska Educational Television Council for Higher Education, Inc., Vol. 3, 1971-72.

MORTON, THOMAS H., and MARIO P. DEI DOLORI. "An Electives Program in a Small High School? It Works!," *English Journal.* Champaign, Illinois: NCTE, Vol. 60, No. 7 (October, 1971).

MULLER, HERBERT J. *The Uses of English.* New York: Holt, Rinehart & Winston, Inc., 1967.

OLSON, PAUL A., and FRANK M. RICE (eds.). "Introduction," *A Curriculum for English, Grade One.* Lincoln, Nebraska: University of Nebraska Press, 1967.

_____. *Language Explorations for the Elementary Grades*. Lincoln, Nebraska: University of Nebraska Press, 1967.

_____. "The Rhetoric of Literature, Units 71 and 72" and "The Rhetoric of Literature, Unit 89," *A Curriculum for English*. Lincoln, Nebraska: University of Nebraska Press, 1968-69.

ROBERTS, PAUL. *English Sentences*. New York: Harcourt, Brace and World, 1962. Chapter 19.

SMILEY, MARJORIE. "Teacher's Manual," *Gateway English*. New York: The Macmillan Company. Pp. 1 ff.

SMITH, JACK E., JR. "180 Days: Observation of an Elective Year," *English Journal*. Champaign, Illinois: NCTE, Vol. 60, No. 2 (February, 1971).